THE GRACES OF CHRISTMAS

Drawings by Frank Kacmarcik

BERNARD WUELLNER, S.J.

THE
GRACES
OF
CHRISTMAS

The Bruce Publishing Company
Milwaukee

IMPRIMI POTEST:

Leo D. Sullivan, S.J.
Praepositus Provincialis
Provinciae Detroitensis

NIHIL OBSTAT:

John A. Schulien
Censor librorum

IMPRIMATUR:

✠ Albertus G. Meyer
Archiepiscopus Milwauchiensis

die 26a Maii, 1958

The Library of Congress catalog entry for this book
appears at the end of the text.

INTRODUCTION

The shower of divine favors that gladdens our lives at Christmas time seems to contain many different graces. Each of these deserves loving reflection and prayerful pondering. At this season the soul joins Mary and Joseph in a joyous feasting on these mysterious truths and blessings of the Christian religion. The spirit seems to respond to the Holy Spirit more by appreciation, desire, and giving than by much eagerness to ask.

Grace is used in this little book in its wide theological sense of any divine supernatural gift. Its meanings here include Christ Himself, sanctifying grace, interior actual graces in man's spiritual powers, and exterior divine helps for the soul's salvation and growth.

Scriptural phrases which do not exactly follow the Douay-Rheims version are not put in quotation marks, even though they are close to the wording of the version and closely follow the Vulgate. This familiar use of well-known lines helps to attract attention to certain details which longer, exact citation of an aging translation might leave blurred before our notice.

These Christmas thoughts and prayers are little gifts of the heart to the Heart in the cradle of Bethlehem. Those who regularly practice mental prayer will know how to cast them into the formal methods of preparation, preludes, and points to which they are accustomed.

May one of Christ's graces to us this year be an intimate understanding of the many graces of His birth.

CONTENTS

THE GRACES OF CHRISTMAS

1. THE GRACE OF SONSHIP

A Son Is Given to Us

The best Christmas gift comes to us from God and Mary. This gift is God's Son and Mary's Son. The great fact of His Godhead towers over all other realities that attend Christ's birth. This truth of the Incarnation declares that the Second Person in God has become man, that God and man are united in the one person of the divine Son, and that the Infant on Mary's arm is truly God as well as truly man.

1

The main purpose of Christ's coming is related to this fact of His divine sonship. The Son is given to us. He has come not merely to tour the earth and to make us better and happier people. He has become a son of man principally to make us sons of God] The fine gift of our graced sonship and of brotherhood with Him is to be the fruit of His redeeming work for us.

Divine sonship naturally appears as the principal theme of the Christmas Masses, and especially of the first or midnight Mass. The Church would have us renew our faith, hope, love, and joy as we again meet Christ. Uniting with the thoughts of this Mass, the children of the Church renew their belief in this pivotal article of the Christian creed: We believe in Jesus Christ, God's only Son, our Lord, who was conceived by the Holy Spirit and born of the Virgin Mary. In this belief in the dual sonship of the Saviour, the Christian proclaims his glorious answer to challenging heretics, doubters, and unbelievers. Christmas begins for us with this triumphant Credo: the true Son of God is also truly son of Mary.

The new event that occurred in time in Palestine was not Christ's becoming God or becoming the Son of His eternal Father. Divinity and sonship are His forever and forever within the Blessed Trinity. What is new is God's becoming man. This human nature, miraculously conceived in a virgin without a human father, by the power of the Holy Spirit, and miraculously delivered by an immaculate mother, is new. The Child newly born is not a mixture of God and man. He is at once fully God and fully man, whole and entire in His own nature, and whole and entire in our human nature. The bond of union is the Second Person of God. Hence, this incarnation of enfleshment of God is a two-in-one mystery, the nature of God and the nature of man made one in the person of God's

Son. He has a divine name, the Word, the Son of God; He has a human name, Christ, Jesus of Nazareth, the Son of Mary. Both names refer to the same one Person who possesses and preserves intact both His eternal unchangeable nature and His time-born changeable nature.

Gabriel, that majestic ambassador, on the day of the Annunciation had told Mary that this is the way it would be. The holy one to be born of you will be called the Son of God, Son of the most high and holy God.[1] Your son will be God's Son.

Elizabeth also seems to have known this truth by heaven-sent insight. She knew that her cousin was carrying a child, who nevertheless was a divine Child. In humble surprise at Mary's gracious visit she cried out: How is it that this favor is done to me that the mother of my Lord should come to me?[2]

St. John adopted the title, the Word, as the name of the divine Son. In his prologue he has perhaps made the best of all statements of the divinity of the Master whom he knew so well. In the very beginning was the Word. The Word abided with God. The Word was God. . . . The Word created all things. . . . And the Word was made flesh and dwelt among us. His glory we have seen, the glory of the only-begotten of the Father, full of grace and truth.[3]

John's phrase about the "Word made flesh" in declaring the twofold nature of the divine Person is the source of all those beautiful paradoxes which we love to recall at the Christmas season. Since the one Person possesses all attributes of both His natures, we may simultaneously assert both divine and human traits of Him. It is literally true that Mary's Babe is her Creator. Man's Maker is made man. Omnipotence is in bonds. The strong might of God belongs to this frail mite. The Infant whose hands

cannot reach the heads of the shaggy cattle in His stable
has flung forth the brilliant billions of the stars at his
creative fiat. He who feeds the hungry millions of the
birds Himself hungers for His mother's milk. The unbeginning God is born anew in time; the Ancient of days is
but an hour old. He is the everlasting Man.[4] The King
of Heaven has become a slave on earth;[5] our very Lord
is now serving us and the Lawgiver of the universe begins
obeying His mother. The Owner of the heavens has only
a swath of linen as His recognized property on earth. That
fragile finite beauty belongs to the uncreated splendor of
God. God the Giver and God the Gift lies cradled in
hay before our shining eyes.

Pope St. Leo I, who championed this double sonship
of Jesus Christ at a crisis in the Church's history, shows
the delight of the believer's mind in the mystery.

As the uniqueness of each nature was preserved and combined in one person, His majesty took on our lowliness, His
strength assumed our weakness, His eternity made His own
our mortality. . . .

Thus, the Son of God enters this lowly world, coming down
from His heavenly throne without departing from His Father's
glory, now generated in a new order by a new nativity. He is
generated in a new order: for, though invisible in His own
nature, He has become visible in our nature; the immeasurable
One willed to be limited; and while remaining all that He
was before all time, He began to exist in time. Around His
boundless majesty the Lord of the universe threw a shadow
and took on the likeness of a slave. The impassible God did not
disdain to become a man subject to suffering; the immortal God
did not shrink from the laws of death. He is generated in a new
birth, for inviolate virginity without carnal desire supplied the
material of His flesh. Her nature He took from the mother
of God, but not our human fault. The miracle of His birth
from a virgin's womb does not make the nature of our Lord
Jesus Christ different from ours. For He who is true God is
also true man. . . .[6]

The Power to Become Sons of God

Our wonderment over His divine sonship increases when we realize that He has come to share His sonship with us and to make us by the adoption of grace children of His own eternal Father and brothers of Himself. For this is the third form of sonship which Christmas recalls. Christ is Son of God from eternity; Christ is son of Mary since Nazareth and Bethlehem; we, too, are sons or are meant to be transformed into sons of God by receiving the spiritual nature of sanctifying grace.

This third sonship, our supernatural sonship, is as true as are the other two for Christ. The Son of God, His Apostles, and His Church are ever teaching it. St. John glowingly connected it with Christ's sonship in his prologue. He came to His own, though His own did not receive Him. But to those who received Him and believed in Him He gave the power to become the sons of God, to be men who are born not just of blood and flesh and human will, but men born of God. Of the fullness of His grace and truth we have all received, grace upon grace.[7] In his Epistle, John tells us that because we are born of God, we are called sons, and truly are sons.[8] Because we are sons, our Lord taught us to address God as our Father in heaven. Because the grace of baptism is a gift of new godlike life, Christ spoke of this sacrament as a new birth in water — to the astonishment of Nicodemus. If we are sons, St. Paul continues, then we are also heirs, heirs of God, heirs to heaven which is our Father's home and estate. As favored sons, we are, says St. Peter, "sharers in the divine nature,"[9] participating in it by the renewing, uplifting, and transfiguring gift of sanctifying grace. God loves us as His sons and as brothers of His only-begotten Son, His Son by nature, Jesus Christ.

Even when we sin against our Father, He welcomes us
back as truant sons and not as wayward hired help. As
adopted members of the divine family, as God's friends
with a graced nearness to Him, as united in mystical union
with Christ's Church, we can by good deeds merit more
grace and love and fuller eternal rewards from our heavenly
Father, Christ's Father and our Father.

Historians of the Mass texts report that the prayer read
daily at the mingling of the wine and water during the
Offertory comes from the very ancient Roman Mass for
Christmas Day.[10] It clearly connects Christ's becoming a
son of man and our becoming sons of God, while wine
and water united symbolize our union with Christ. "O
God, who wonderfully created human nature in its dignity
and still more wonderfully refashioned it, grant us through
this mystery [of the mixture] of the wine and water to
become sharers of the godhead of Him who deigned to
become a participant in our humanity."

Our Holy Father, Pius XII, considered this same truth
of sonship to be the leading thought of the faithful at
the annual renewal of Christmas.

> With the coming of the birthday of the Redeemer, the Church
> would bring us to Bethlehem's cave and there teach us that we
> must be born again and undergo a complete reformation. That
> will happen only when we are intimately and vitally united
> to the Word of God made man and participate in His divine
> nature, to which we have been elevated.[11]

If we could see our souls radiant with grace, we would
know the splendor and dignity to which divine sonship
raises us. But really, what could raise our appreciation of
this Christmas gift more than the fact that the Son of
God thought it worth His descent to earth chiefly to give
us this life of sonship? The creative Fountain of grace
came to pour out His grace, His presence, His divinity,

His sonship, and His filial inheritance upon all whom His Father had selected to share it.

Be Followers of God, as Most Dear Children

Only sons of grace can celebrate Christmas well. Only sons of God are ready to keep company with the Son of God and son of Mary. Christmas, the day and season of grace, follows Advent, the time of preparing for the grace. Being prepared, the children of God spend Christmas in the state of grace; they give joyous thanks to their Father for sending His Son to give them sonship; they do the good deeds of grace. Christmas is a fortnight of joyous prayer to a Father who loved us sinners and a time of spiritual yearning that the will of our Father in heaven may be done on earth. As sons of God, we hold Him in filial love and present to Him noble sons' reverence for His kind, strong will. We know that He cares for us and we trust ourselves to His fatherly government.

Christmas renews our desires to please our Father by becoming better sons. Christmas repeats to us the importance of helping others in our home and circle to find, keep, and advance in the grace of God.

Our sonship helps us to recognize better how just is that startling advice of Christ: Be ye perfect as your heavenly Father is perfect.[12] St. Paul has reworded it: Be followers of God, as most dear children.[13] Fathers can well be proud of sons and daughters who copy their virtues and walk in their pathways. The best compliment, the best thanks, and the best love that we can show our Father is to make ourselves like Him in the virtues He practices toward us. His Son has told us what those virtues are: thoughtfulness, mercy, helpful gifts at every turn, and ever faithful love. *Noblesse oblige!* A nobleman's obligations are not mere debts, but privileges which he honors.

Our Father in heaven, make us worthy sons of Yours. Guide us to live as Your divine Son lived for You.

Christ, the Son of God, we give deepest thanks to You for coming to make us sons of God. Christ, full of grace, fill us with Your grace.

Mother of Christ and Mother of Divine Grace, Mother of the Christ who is the first divine grace, pray that we may be sons of yours, through your Son's grace.

2. THE GRACE OF A HEAVENLY VISIT

He Descended From Heaven

These words of the Nicene Creed used in the Mass tell us about another grace of Christmas. Christmas is the memorial of the day when God showed His friendship to men by coming down the long stairs from heaven to visit us on our earth. Christmas recalls the divine answer to the prayers of patriarchs, prophets, and all holy men and women that God Himself would graciously come. One of the seasonal hymns tells us that

9

From paradise to earth he came
that we with Him might dwell.

After Adam and Eve had tried to expel God from His
own garden and their lives, He made a firm promise that
some one born of woman would come to undo the evil.
During centuries He renewed His divine pledge again and
again. Human spirits invited this Messias, this expected
anointed one. Surely He was needed. Surely the thousands
of years of preparation for His coming should have been
enough to sharpen human longing and prepare human
hearts. Whom would God send? The Messias would be
some one very special. But few, if any, even guessed that
it would be God Himself who would enter our world.

The long, long years of waiting tended more to prove
men's desperate need than to fit us better to receive Him.
Even the meaning of the divine promise became distorted;
and the twisted interpretation accented more our need of
heavenly help to see things aright. When at last heaven
and earth were so near on that December night which
opened Christ's era, when the invisible God became visible
in a human infant's features, who were ready for Him and
who welcomed Him?

Only a few seem to have been ready. Mary and Joseph,
the infant John the Baptist, Anna and Simeon, some
shepherds and some strangers from other lands, and, perhaps, in some dumb way, the ox and ass recognized the
Master of creation. High and low in Israel did not know
their God. He came unto His own; His own did not
welcome Him.[14] There was no room for Him in the inn,
small as He was! They were ready for a great lord of this
world. Their fancies were expecting a mighty conqueror
with armies. They were awaiting an economic reformer to
lead them into lands filled with coins and silks. Because
of their foolish earthly ambitions, their hearts had mis-

read the divine promises, and they were completely taken by surprise. When the Splendor of the Father's glory appeared, they did not see Him and could not recognize Him even when He identified Himself by His charity and miracles.

To His mother and those ready for Him, He brought a breath of heavenly fragrance, a glimpse of celestial beauty, and the perfection of divine holiness. The cave of Bethlehem became a miniature heaven on earth. "The goodness and kindness of God our Savior has appeared."[15] St. Paul here reports the delight of those who recognized Him as God of heaven and earth. He has come not as an armed emperor, not as a calculating inspector of tax accounts, and not as a judge of His enemies, He has come in the friendly graciousness of a child who wants to win friends. We have seen Him! exclaimed St. John.[16] Now, Lord, Your servant may die in peace, for my eyes have seen Your Salvation, exclaimed Simeon.[17] "Let heaven rejoice, and let earth leap with joy, for He has truly come," is the prompting of the Offertory text.

WELCOMING THE HEAVENLY VISITOR

Life is to be a continuous preparation for the coming of Christ. At many moments of life this shining Personality steps down from heaven and enters our lives. Each of His advents is a fresh opportunity for gladly welcoming Him.

We must get ourselves ready for His appearances. For He will come when He wills. Wherever He is, whenever He appears, however He comes, whatever the disguise He wears, we must be set to welcome Him.

Having once come to earth, the heavenly Visitor comes again and again. He comes again annually in the liturgical renewal of His life in the mysteries of the Christmas season. Glad at His coming, we run with shepherds to see Him and race with the swift Magi to adore Him. At Christmas services and in the Christmas Divine Office we greet Him again as Zachary did: Blessed is the Lord God of Israel, for He has visited His people and brought them redemption.[18] We open all the locks which selfishness has put on our hearts, for we want Him to enter. We cleanse the stables of our consciences of all foul sin. We offer to Him what little we have that He would take it as His own and use it for His purposes while He stays with us on earth.

Catholic peoples of different lands have developed various customs to assure Christ that He is welcome in their hearts and in their homes at Christmas time. In Ireland and Wales the latch at every cabin is open so that Mary and Joseph may come in with the Child or that any stranger substituting for Christ may enter. The Poles keep a vacant chair for Mary and Christ at their Christmas Eve supper. Many light a candle in the window to say to the earth-visiting feet of God: "Come in, we have been looking for You to come. You have been promised to us. You are needed. You are welcome in this inn. Our home is decorated for Your coming. Our bodies are dressed in festive style. Our souls are decked with virtues. Do not wait longer. Do not knock. Come in, Christ, come in."

But Christmas Day is only one of His visiting days. Time after time He speeds to us from heaven in the Consecration of the Mass. We welcome Him: "Blessed is He who has come in the name of the Lord." Each morning He waits to be welcomed into our ready bodies and souls if only we will accept Him in Holy Communion. He would make our hearts His cradle; He would steep our spirits, like Mary's, in wondering love; the Word made flesh would make us welcome. All day He lingers in our tabernacles, waiting for our visits to the Blessed Sacrament. It should be enough to know that He is there. We should need no special angelic message to go over and see this Wonder dwelling in our own city.

He appears among us in other guises, too. He comes to us in the teachings and orders of the Holy Father and of our bishops. He makes His presence felt in the commands of our legitimate superiors in church, state, and family. He comes to us in the members of His Church, His Mystical Body, and especially in our needy fellow men. When I was a stranger, you took Me in. When I was sick, you visited Me,[19] the heavenly Visitor shall say to the imitators of His charity at the hour of their judgment. He comes to us in a client seeking aid, in a new child in the family, in a mourner needing sympathy, in a sinner needing mercy, and in an enemy seeking a forgiving smile.

He comes to us, too, in many little personal inspirations. These are actual graces consisting of thoughts, desires, and resolutions that flow through our minds and wills in the course of each day. They suggest a truth, they remind us of His presence, they strengthen our wills, they prompt to a good deed, they keep us out of trouble, they help us to prudent decisions. They come in our reading and in our prayer. They come when we see some good example of another or are pained by evil done by another. The graces come when we seek them and when we have not sought them. But in a life governed by God's love, they come often. In all these movements of mind and will, Christ is at work in our lives. Among the more important are the heavenly desires which He makes us experience. When the Lord of Heaven comes into our lives, we are flooded with love of the good things of

Christ and of heaven. For He is lifting up our hearts and
minds; He is prompting us to devote time to prayer, to
bring ourselves closer to God, to increase God's glory, to
receive Him in Holy Communion, to purify our consciences better, to do His will on earth as it is done in
heaven. He pours into us eager hope that the light and joy
of the Kingdom of Christ may spread through all the
world, that all men may know God and Jesus Christ sent
by God. These desires, condensed in the Our Father, mark
the presence of the heavenly Visitor, more and more lifting our spirits upward to heaven. By cherishing these
desires and starting to act on them, we give pleasant com-
radeship to the heavenly Visitor. Of this interior coming of
Christ, the Church reminds us in the third Mass at
Christmas: He has appeared, teaching us to give up worldly
desires and to live in a godly way in this world.[20]

HOSTS AND HOSTESSES

The life of grace in our souls seems to have two phases:
periods of waiting and periods of welcoming — times of
longing preparations and times of joyous possession. We
are often called upon to act as hosts or hostesses to the
divine Visitor. We need no elaborate etiquette and instruction in it to welcome Him well. But we do need the habit
of readiness for His company and warmth in our hospitality to Him. A sincere, sinless, and prayerful life is
preparation enough. We must keep pressing Him, too, to
come whenever He pleases, not only on formal occasions
but in surprising casual calls also. We must assure Him
that we should like Him to come on His terms, by day
or night, with a gift for us if He wishes or with a request
for our help if He would like it. Life, then, may become
a perpetual advent of longing for Him. But when we yearn

for Him, we know that He means to come. When our hearts and minds reach high up to heaven, we will meet the heavenly Visitor on His way down to our souls; and then we rejoice exceedingly, for He is with us.

Some day He will come for more than a visit. Some day He will come to take us home forever.

> Sudden as sweet
> Come the expected feet.
> All joy is young and new all art,
> And He, too, Whom we have by heart.[21]

There will be little to fear from the Judge for whose coming we have been yearning.[22] Our first visit to heaven will be an everlasting homecoming.

3. THE GRACE OF A REDEEMER

CHRIST THE SAVIOUR IS BORN!

"Silent Night" and other Christmas carols are filled with happy echoes of the joyful tidings which the angels trumpeted to the herders of the flocks. The angelic spokesman gave the reason why the human watchmen should rejoice: Today a Saviour who is Christ the Lord is born for you.[23] This message restates what the angel had already told His Mother and Joseph: His name shall be called Jesus, for He shall save His people from their sins.[24]

God selected the name in view of His Son's office or commission on earth. Today the newborn Child is beginning His work of salvation. Today the promised seed of the woman starts to crush the evil serpent. He is the sinless One come to conquer sin. He is the Man full of grace, come to dispense grace. He is the Saviour come to salvage the good and the possibilities for good that still remained in the world. This Liberator will free His people from their bondage to evil, strike from them the many chains of slavery to the world, the flesh, the self, and the devil. He is to make earth safe for human souls and open heaven to them. He will remake men, and they will remake their institutions for the better security of souls. He is the new Prince of a new kingdom wherein God and men are at peace with each other, but He must present His own body and soul to be our peace offering. He is the Judge offering His own humanity as our bond and payment to divine justice. With the great ransom of His precious blood and love for God paid in our name, He tenders full pardon for all human faults and crimes. He is the divine Healer come to cure all our old wounds of the spirit and to deliver us from all the miseries due to the diseases of our sins.

He is Saviour both as Good Shepherd of souls and as Lamb of God. It was fitting that the Good Shepherd should call other shepherds to His side this birthnight, for they could understand a shepherd ready to lay down His life for His sheep. It was in keeping with His life's dedication that the Lamb of God who is to be slain for sinners should come to a spot where the lambs for Temple sacrifices were born and pastured. How wonderfully apt is the divine sense of symbolism that finds shepherds and lambs near the Saviour's manger. Heroic men and unprotesting lives for holocaust; givers and gifts; men and things whose existence was centered in sacrifice to the All-Holy.

"For us and for our salvation He descended from heaven and became flesh of the Holy Spirit and the Virgin Mary and was made man." These words of the Mass link the Incarnation of God with His saving purpose. For this Son of Mary is both high priest and victim of the new sacrifice willed by God. He is already anointed by His personal union with divinity; and as anointed, He is the Christ. In His human nature, He is our Mediator, dear to God and dear to us, able to restore friendship between God and man, for He is both God and Man. When John the Baptist saw Him, he knew Him as the destined Victim of redemption: Behold the Lamb of God, the one who takes away the sins of the world![25] True to the dedication given Him when He received His name as Jesus, He saved us at a great price, His own infinitely precious blood. His sacrifice and our ransom will be the pains of His human body, the wounds of His flesh, the blood of His heart, the penitential anguish of His spirit, and His obedient love offered to God. His Father will accept His own Son's offering and hear His pleas for our sake. We will be redeemed, for we have a divine Redeemer.

We believe. We hope in this wonderful little Saviour. We admit that the angel said justly: This is joyful news that Christ our Saviour is born.

O the Success of His Redemption![26]

The delights of Christmas include both our knowledge of God's goodness in sending His own Son to save us and our bright hope that we are counted among those who have joined the band of His redeemed. It is so wonderful to know that the benefits of His redeeming presence, work, and love are meant for us.

Sometimes when looking at the crib, we may think that it is a place only for glorious, holy beings like Mary, Joseph, and the angels. But when we remember that He is the Saviour, we know that it is the place also for us sinners. The crowds of adorers must include us, for "I have not come to call the just, but sinners."[27] He desires us to come, to lay His little hand of tender pardon on our heads, and to hear our gasping plea for mercy. Sinners belong here, for He is the Saviour of all men.

It is good that we are welcome to His presence, for in spiritual matters we always were and always are helpless without Him. For all that pertains to saving souls, men absolutely need Him. Men do not give themselves God's grace. Sinners do not reform themselves; the helpless are unable to help themselves. No one begins to turn to God or aspire to heaven without God's previous gift. In the things of the spirit and in the realm of grace all men are like the dying who need the aid of the living and transfusions of living blood. "Without Me," Christ later told His Apostles, "you can do nothing."[28] The more desperate we know our plight to have been, the more profound will be our appreciation of His redeeming help. He alone rescues us from misery in time and horror in eternity.

The goodness and kindness of God our Saviour has appeared;[29] in gracious mercy His majesty and justice have now been veiled. If we respond lovingly to His goodness and kindness, our sins will disappear. How good and kind He is shines out not only in the winsome beauty of His coming as an Infant, but also in the amazing initiative of His coming. For He appeared when we were yet His enemies, before we wanted Him, at the time when His love knew that we stood in much need of Him even though we would cruelly ignore or rebuff Him. This cradle

of Christ is the cradle of our great human hope. Since
the sacred earth of Bethlehem has held the holy body of
the Babe of Mary, there is no more room for despair on
earth. Our spirits must exult with Mary's in God our
Saviour. For in giving His Son to be our Redeemer, God
with Him has given us all things that are permanently
worth while.

The grounds for our convinced hope in Him stand solid.
The grace of hope includes the abiding habitual disposition
and the acts whereby we expect from God both the means
to our salvation and the entrance of our redeemed souls
into heaven. Why should we not hope in Christ? The
Redeemer has everything we need. Christ has promised
everything. Christ has died to make everything possible
and available to us. Christ has opened heaven, and is the
redemptive door held open to us.

He has infinite loyalty to keep glorious promises. He has
the infinite goodness from which to dispense ends and
means to us. His is the blood in which we are redeemed.
One drop of it would have been enough to win mercy
for all men's sins and to pay for all graces, but His blood
flowed to the last drop for us. His is the treasury of merits
on which we draw. His is the boundless power, too, to do
all that He has promised. His is the provident, intelligent
plan for our salvation. His providence is personal. His plan
is complete. His wisdom has overlooked no item of our
needs. In addition, Christ's farseeing genius invented the
Church to keep the truth of God and the means of grace
ever at our disposal. His is the fidelity that proved Himself
faithful to the striking challenges of His own predictions
and promises. His love beckoning us to heaven wills that
we, His saved ones, should forever be His glory and that
we, His flock, should be forever near the Shepherd of
our souls.

The Mother of the Redeemer composed her rapturous poem praising Him before His birth:

> My soul exalts the Lord,
> My spirit exults in God my Saviour.[30]

Zachary chanted of His mercies at the birth of John, His forerunner. The Church for centuries has used as her Matins and Vesper hymn the Ambrosian lines, set to such splendid music by the great organist, Pietro Yon, in our century: *Jesu, Redemptor omnium* or the *Gesu Bambino.*

> Jesus, the Ransomer of man,
> Who, ere created light began,
> Didst from the sovereign Father spring,
> His power and glory equalling.
>
> Salvation's Author, call to mind
> How, taking form of humankind,
> Born of a Virgin undefiled,
> Thou in man's flesh becam'st a Child.
>
> And we who, by Thy precious blood
> From sin redeemed, are marked for God,
> On this the day that saw Thy birth
> Sing the new song of ransomed earth.[31]

We would please the Child Redeemer if we would make these Christian hopes our own. Redeemer of the world, count us among Your redeemed. Lamb of God, take away our sins. Jesus, Jesus, be to us a Jesus, and save us. Shepherd of souls, help us; for while we can do nothing without You, with You we can do all things.

Mary, our life, our sweetness, and our hope, pray for us that we may become worthy of the wonderful promises of your Son.

4. THE GRACE OF THE KING

The newly born Christ came, as He had been announced, as the King of men.

His Jewish people had long been expecting a new kingdom or a new leader who would begin a new era of splendor and blessings. Nine months before, Gabriel had told His Mother that her Son would be a great man who would forever reign in the house of David. Elizabeth had known that Mary's unborn Son was to be her Lord.

22

The chorusing angels had told the shepherds that the Person of whom they sang and spoke was Christ the Lord. The wise men, themselves kings, came in search of the newborn King of the Jews. Years later Jesus would go about proclaiming His kingdom, talking of it in parables. After entering into Jerusalem in regal triumph, this humble King, would die for His kingship, His kingdom, and the people of His realm. Before the Jewish religious court, He fearlessly affirmed His divine sonship, and died for that. Before Pilate, He stood firm on His kingship.

> Art thou a king, then?
> Yes; as you say, I am. My kingdom, though, is not of this world. I am a king, come to bear witness to the truth.[32]

He deserves a noble salute from us, then, today on His birthday as our King.

We human beings are the subjects of this King who reigns from crib and cross. We have the deepest need for the King and His kingdom for our soul's well-being. We need a King to show us the way. We need His authority to guide and command us, and to organize our spiritual endeavors. We need a King to free us from our enemies, to help us fight for the right, to protect us for the future, and to animate our courage. We need a King to put order into our lives and maintain us in peaceful security. We need a King to bring us together into an effective spiritual unit and to establish a firm society, ruled by Him, for the realization of human spiritual good. We need this King's personal example to inspire and motivate us. We need to share in the spiritual treasures of our King. We need His power to end our drifting, our anarchy, our injustice, our panic. We need a King to march before us, with a cause, a plan, a goal, a hope, a personality, an organization, and a united love such as only a great divine Leader with a great divine cause can supply to us.

To meet all these needs of ours, Christ our King has come and put Himself, under His Father's orders, at the head of the human race and at the head of His Church. He will reign forever. To the end of time He is King of all the good on earth. Throughout eternity He is King of angels and of the redeemed in heaven.

The titles to this majestic lordship over men are well known. There is more to His royal prerogative than the mere fact that He was descended from the family of the great King David's line. In his divine nature He is naturally superior to all men. In His human nature He has been sent by His Father with a royal anointing — the Christ who captains all men in their advance to heaven by their service of God on earth. All power has been given to Him in heaven and on earth. He has the power to make laws, to command, and to judge. He is King, too, by the sheer height of His wisdom and charity, by His ascendancy over all others in mind, will, and grace.

No wonder that crib figures, paintings, and statues of the Infant of Prague often represent Him wearing a crown. For He is King of all kings, the Lord of all lords, Jesus Christ, the divine King.

Mary at Bethlehem gave Him not only the divine adoration which He deserved, but also the royal homage which He claimed. It seems to us, too, peculiarly fitting that shepherds and Magi should come to His manger. A shepherd of the flock was a common ancient name for a royal leader, especially of pastoral people. The Magi very likely were kings, for there are several indications of this. Isaias speaks of the gift-bearing kings of Araby and other far lands, and St. Matthew narrates their direct approach to King Herod for information, in the manner of kings dealing with their equals, and indicates royal gifts and courtly manners in their approach to the infant King.

It was appropriate that these kings should come to bow before the greatest King of all and to put themselves under His rule. When they came to Herod, what did they expect? A son lately born in Herod's palace? How much better was their real discovery, how much lovelier and kinglier to find the Infant throned on His Mother's lap!

One facet of the many-splendored gift of Christmas is God's goodness in meeting our great need of a king and giving us the noblest possible King in the person of His own Son. He comes with a divinely sealed promise that His kingdom shall never end. His position as King is secure as long as His kingdom shall endure: on earth to the consummation of time, in heaven as long as the redeemed rejoice with their Prince.

My Kingdom Is Not of This World!

One of the persistent problems of Christ's life was the Jewish misunderstanding of the nature of His kingdom. Most of the Jews thought it must be an earthly kingdom with pomp and power, wealth and honors, treasuries and armories, courtiers and legions. It would be a kingdom purified of pagan idolatry, but, after all, just one more Alexandrian or Roman empire. Pilate perhaps came closest to understanding that this Man before his court did not fight with military weapons and that His revolution was purely interior in the realms of truth and loyalties. Herod the Great feared the little infant King as a potential earthly rival and, therefore, plotted to do away with Him. He could not grasp that "He who gives away eternal kingdoms does not despoil men of temporal realms."[33] Even Christ's Apostles had not grasped the nature of Christ's kingdom on the day that they accompanied Him to the mount of His Ascension.

What would Christ want with a petty kingdom like Herod's or with petty temporal might like Rome's? His kingdom is far vaster. His is a kingdom of the things of the spirit. He is King of minds by truth and of wills by justice, peace, and love. He is the royal Victor over sin. His imperial glory is in the grace of the soul. His ambition is not the material prize of world lordship that Satan offered Him, but the joyous reward of doing the will of God on earth. His visible kingdom is in the organization and membership of His Church, built on the amazing strength that He put into the frail rock known as Peter.

His jurisdiction reaches to all men in all centuries since His coming. It penetrates all the days of their lives, from birth and baptism up to and beyond the grave into their days in heaven.

He is the King of hearts. He is the center of all high spiritual affections. He is the Man who will claim and win fuller loyalty than all others who have ever lived. The brave will honor Him as King of martyrs; the pure will honor Him as Crown of virgins; the wise will honor Him as Source of truth.

He is the King of gifts. He is the Prince of peace. He is the Heart of love. He comes to be with His people because He loves them. He comes to share His grace, happiness, and virtue with His own. He comes to shed His blood for each of His people. He comes to die even for His opponents' salvation. He is the King whom even children know as their royal Brother.

This is the King whom the Gentile kings found resting on the precious throne of His queen-mother, guarded only by the kindly eyes of His foster father and the vigilant friendship of nearby shepherds. They tell us what to do. Fall down and adore. Honor, praise, and wonder at His royalty. Seek and search for Him. Where is He that is born King of the Jews? For we have seen His star in the East and have come to adore.[34] He is the great King; the greatest of us must salute Him and serve under Him. For to serve so great a king is to be a king. *Cui servire regnare est.*

THY KINGDOM COME!

To lay our crowns, our honors, our talents, and all our treasures at His feet, to acclaim His kingship, and to pledge our eternal loyalty to Him are ways in which we can join the three kings in their homage. We hail Him in the Church's prayers and songs: in the *Gloria*, "Lord God, seated at the right hand of the Father"; in the *Sanctus*, echoing His royal entry into Jerusalem: "Blessed is He who comes in the name of the Lord"; in the *Te Deum* of thanksgiving, "Thou are the Christ, the King of Glory"; in the ancient processional applause: "Christ is reigning, Christ is triumphant, Christ is our sovereign."

We thank Him that He has selected us to believe in Him and follow Him. We are pleased and proud that by baptism He has transferred us from the old dominion of Satan into the kingdom of His light and love. We are grateful that by confirmation His Spirit has anointed us to be witnesses to His kingship and soldiers crusading for His cause and person.

Humbly and gladly and wholeheartedly we offer ourselves anew to His service. We beg Him to be King and Master of our souls, and to capture and rule us completely. We request Him to accept our persons, our loves, our loyalties, our fortunes, our ambitions, our lives, our families, our nation as His own: Take our hearts and reign in them and make them like Your heart. Be our King and lead us where You will.

We pray for the glory of His Kingdom: Thy Kingdom come! King of men, at Your new coming this Christmas, bring with You the great graces that are needed that Your kingdom may spread more widely among unbelievers and may grow more deeply in Your present servants. May Your truth spread like morning light drenching the lands. May Your Church grow like the mustard seed. May Your will be better known and Your royal laws better respected. May Your love bind together all men of good will. May Your glory shine in the virtues of old and young. May Your peace reign in all hearts. May Your hopes for men come true. May Your Sacred Heart be King of all hearts.

5♦ THE GRACE OF SPIRITUAL CHILDHOOD

GOD IN MARY'S ARMS

The wonder never ceases that the God of majesty came as a frail human child.

This fact of the divine infancy contains a great grace, a great lesson, and a great hope for us.

To Isaias' prophetic eye, He was the Child who would be born to us. To the searching shepherds, the sign was a swaddled infant. To the delight of the magi, the newborn King at the tip of the huge star's beam was a little Hebrew boy clasped in Mary's arms. Though He was miraculously born, there was no miracle about the human helplessness which her motherly love must help. Her spotless hands must bathe and wrap His tiny body. Her immaculate milk must feed Him. Her pure lips must sing His cradle songs. He was a very little baby, as she and Joseph knew Him.

With them we believe, we adore, and we wonder. We can make St. Bernard's exclamation our own: "Great is the Lord and greatly to be praised. Little is the Lord and greatly to be loved."

Our minds keep returning to the puzzle of His reasons for becoming our very small Brother. Some of the graces and teachings of this divine infancy seem clear. We know that God is a poet in love with the world. He sends His Son in the infinitely gracious form of a winsome child. We know that Christ wished to become man in all things except sin and that He longed to practice the virtues of all stages of human life. Therefore, He volunteered to be a child for all men. In humility He took the form of a child, the nature of a slave, and the duties of a completely dependent creature. Since He had infused knowledge of His redemptive mission, He practiced the virtues of infancy consciously and deliberately. He would be the model of a child's devotedness to parents, of simplicity in being cared for by older people, of lowliness of mind in admitting that His parents were His superiors deserving obedience and trust. His infancy would accent His own sweet sinlessness, His willingness to grow and learn, His trust in God's plan and carefulness for His future, His gladness in serving His mother and St. Joseph.

No doubt, He became a child also to be nearer to all children, to the needy, to the poor, and to the dependent serving classes. In dealing with children, He would never forget that He, too, once was an infant and a growing boy. Most of us feel that the Christ Child invented Christmas as a feast for children.

Again, He came as a little one who foresaw Himself preaching in the future that unless we become as little children, we shall not enter into the kingdom of heaven.[35] He would ask wise kings to fall to their knees before Him. For the gate to the kingdom is low; to be a son of God one must also be a child of God. To be great in the realm of Christ, one must become as one of these little ones. This is spiritual childhood. It is a deliberate virtuous response to the grace of divine sonship. It is the proper life of a graced son of God to be like the divine Child.

RALLY OF THE CHILDREN

Children eagerly flock to the side of Christ. In a flash of faith they understand the special message of the Child. They love the Child in the manger and give Him their glad welcome and youthful companionship.

The record shows that, given a chance, children always recognize and love Him. John the Baptist leaped in joy when he and his Lord were still infants in their mothers' wombs. The Holy Innocents of Bethlehem laid down their lives, thereby helping Him make good His escape and live to be the Saviour of all men. They could not sing to Him as angels did. They could not visit Him as shepherds did. They had no precious gifts as Magi had. They could not nurse Him nor dance for Him nor work for Him. They could not play the donkey and carry Him to Egypt. But they could bleed and die for Him.

The children pressed round Him during His public life. He insisted on their being allowed to come near Him. In His great reform of human marriage, Christ was fighting for life, home, and children. He asked His Apostles to forget their ambitions for position in His kingdom and become like young children.

The youthful martyrs have been loyal to Him, their fellow child, their dear God. St. Agnes, the baby martyr in the flames in Japan, and St. Maria Goretti in modern Italy are a few of them. Missionaries know that pagan children are the first to become interested in the religion of Christ. Many of us have seen the piercing happiness of orphans at a Christmas party. What an event, too, is their first Christmas Communion for the innocent young school children in our parishes. Christ and children seem to have a special affinity for each other. At Christmas Mass parents know deep contentment when they see their children coming back from the communion rail with Christ their Friend.

One very young Ohio child, when asked by a whimsical priest whether the Christ Child would have laughed at the long beards and strange garments of the wise men, instantly replied, "No, no, Father; that would have hurt their hearts." That little one knew the heart of the divine little One. Jesus and children understand each other.

UNLESS YOU CHANGE INTO LITTLE CHILDREN

What did Christ mean years later, when He recommended this return to the attitudes, outlooks, and virtues of a child? Why did He see in the young the makings of the members of the kingdom and the heirs of heaven? Why did he prefer children's ideas and ways to those of the Pharisees, the crowds, and even the Apostles?

Certainly our Lord meant to commend something more than mere biological youthfulness, the animal health of the body, the bright eyes and clear skin that contribute to the native sweetness of children, their cuteness and playfulness, their helplessness, and inexperience, their dream worlds and impractical desires, their petulance and impetuosity, and all that we mean by childishness and immaturity. Infinite wisdom was not recommending such mere physical perfections, and much less, any deficiencies or positive faults.

The Master saw other things in children. Their souls still have the unspoiled seeds of virtue implanted in them by God their Maker. They have a spontaneous love for the good and a tender uneasiness about evil. Their untried innocence should be the pattern of the deliberate innocence of older people. Jesus also liked their love of their parents and their spirit of obedience. He liked their attitude of wonder before all the marvels of the world. Why shouldn't the world be wonderful, thinks the child, since a wonderful God made it? Christ liked their recognition of their dependence on others for the goods of this world. He liked their confidence in God's care for them. He liked the hearts still free from attachments to mere riches and pride of place. He liked their docility, their willingness to learn and grow, their freedom from complacency in their attainments. He liked their joy in life. He liked the character in which love still counts for so much. He liked their love of people, of other children, and of animals. He liked their simple ways, their acts, free from pretense, sincere in motive, candid in speech, without meanness in their tactics to reach their ends. No doubt He also was pleased by their direct, plain talk to God in prayer, marked by unclouded faith, by petitions for the big elemental blessings which they know must come from Him, not from themselves, and by glad thanksgiving.

To be a spiritual child, young at heart in the realm of grace, one needs perhaps these three spiritual traits: a continuing ambition for the solid, simple beginner's virtues; lowliness of mind combined with towering aspirations for heavenly things; and childlike attitudes in praying.

The refreshing thing about Berta-Hummel Christmas statuettes and greeting cards is not their coloring and technique, but their child's-eye view of Christ and His friends. These figures have caught the attitudes of children who make the Christ Child one of their own. They bring Him jelly beans and cookies. They put the cow closer to the manger because He will need its milk. They know that He would like to have His dog close by to pat its head. They like to say their night prayers joyously before their God in the manger. No artificial barriers have yet arisen between their praying hearts and the Child who listens and blesses. Even when He does not answer their prayers, they are not surprised that He sometimes says, "No; that isn't good for you. I'll get you something better." God reveals Himself to little ones.

The Servant of the Holy Child

St. Ignatius of Loyola in his *Spiritual Exercises*[36] makes some suggestions for contemplating the persons and deeds connected with the Nativity. One suggestion is to bring ourselves very close to the scene by imagining that we are servants of the Holy Family, attending to some of the needs of Mary, Joseph, and the Child. This leads the soul at prayer to ask: What can we do by way of service to the divine Child? Anyone with genuine Christmas spirit should know the answer.

The Little Flower, St. Thérèse of Lisieux, found her own clear, heroic answer to this Christmas problem. She learned that a great life is made up of little deeds, all of which must be done for Jesus. Her way would be a hidden way to heaven, to steal up to God by innumerable tiny steps. She knew that she would not be able to do great public deeds, initiate great projects in the Church, move the masses by brilliant discourse, perform strenuous penances, or startle a world by her miracles. But she would do what a child could do; she would do all the ordinary things, every day. She would always please the divine Child and never seek to please herself. She would be a genius by taking all the obvious, direct, close-at-hand means to be a saint. She would take the many small opportunities that life's course provided to show her love. She would refuse our Lord nothing. By simple sacrifices, by forgetting self, she would become an image of the divine Child. She knew that violets and crocuses glorify God no less than gorgeous orchids. It all turned out to be an heroic life. God chose to make it the twentieth-century model of spiritual childhood.

Her resulting holiness, of course, was assured from this simple constancy to the little things. For, in love, little things mean very much. The following of the divine Child is truly the imitation of Christ.

St. Joseph, best of all servants of Christ, teach us to serve the Child.

Mother of the divine Child, teach us to be children of yours, daily a little more like your beloved Son. Teach us to love children and to receive them in the name of your Son.[37]

Jesus, meek and humble of heart, make our hearts like Your childlike Heart.

6. THE GRACE OF ADORATION

COME, LET US ADORE HIM!

The Son of God began His human life with an act of loving adoration of His eternal Father.

The Son of God calls to men to come and see His humanity in the manger, to believe in and adore His hidden divinity.

The Church often sends out the same call in the Divine Office of the Nativity and in hymns which she has approved. The opening prayers of Matins burst forth: "Christ

is born for us. Come, let us adore." The glorious chorus
of the *Adeste Fideles* appeals for the same response to
the Christmas truths: "Come, ye believers, behold Him.
Come, let us adore Him, Christ the Lord."

An analysis of all the great paintings of the birth of
Christ would likely reveal scenes of adoration to be the
commonest theme treated. There are adorations by the
Virgin Mother alone with Christ; pictures of Joseph's
adoring lips pressed to the Child's divine feet; adorations
by the Christmas angels, by shepherds old and young, by
the Magi and their retinues; and even the more fanciful
worship of the beasts in the stable before their Master.
Every posture of servants before their creative Lord has
been represented: the doffed caps, the bowed heads, the
curved shoulders, the bent knees, the Oriental prostration,
hands pointed to the Lord in prayer and lifting gifts in
sacrifice, eyes fixed in wonder on the infinite majesty of
the newborn God.

Adoration is a dominant sentiment of the soul at Christmas time. Willingness to adore is a great grace. But only
believers adore. Only the *faithful* know by faith that Christ
is truly the Son of God, true God of true God, begotten,
not created. He deserves adoration; for He is the Second
Person of God become man, the Word made flesh, Son
of both God and Mary. We who believe are glad to adore.

Acts of worship are paid to the divine Person and to His
human nature and its human parts because they are united
with this divine personality. Any act by which direct honor
and reverence are paid to the supreme excellence of God
is adoration. Praise or admiration of Him, thanksgiving
for His goodness to us, simple joy in the fact that He
is God, reverent submission to His lordship, admission
of our need of His help, repentance for our faults, acts
of sacred sacrifice and gift giving to God, and especially

acts of personal love of Him are all varieties of the prayer of adoration. We have heads to bow; we have knees to bring low; we have lips to speak His wonders; we have minds and wills to bring to His service; we have gifts to set aside for Him; we have time to give to Him. We who believe are glad to adore.

The very body and soul of the humanity of Christ deserves this glorification, for it is personally one with the Second Person of God. This is God's flesh and bones, God's face and hands and feet, God's blood and heart, God's human intellect and will. Therefore, says the Church, come, adore Him.

A New Way

Mary's first act of knowing, loving, and praising her divine Son on Christmas introduced into this world an altogether new way of adoring God. Pagans had adored human beings who were not gods. Hebrews, knowing that their God was purely spiritual and inimitable by any created images, had no external presentations of God. Pagans were far from the true God; Hebrews kept Him very sacred yet infinitely remote. But idolatry had a curious fascination for men. Men wanted to have close contact with their god. They wanted to see him and feel him near. Now that the true God has come, they can do so. Come, said the shepherds to each other, let us go over the hills to Bethlehem to see this wonder.[38] We have come, said the kings, with gifts to show that we adore Him.[39]

This adoration of a visible God, of the true God in human flesh, is a totally new conception of religion, of adoration, and of prayer. Now that in His person a totally new link has been forged between God and men, a totally new response of the human spirit to the demands of the divine becomes appropriate. Christ Himself is the first

manifestation of the incarnational or sacramental principle
in religion. The material, the finite, the human, the non-
divine is made sacred by the choice of God; it becomes
a means of contact and union of man with God; it lifts
men up to God and no longer casts them far from Him.
The Preface of the Christmas Mass tells it in a lovely
line: "Through Him, whom we know by sight, we are
drawn to love of things invisible." The theology of the
sacraments uses the same theme; for sensible things as
water, bread, oil, and human words, become the signs and
carriers of divine grace to the soul. God has wedded heaven
and earth, for He has sent His heavenly Son to earth.

Moments of Adoration

One lesson that we are glad to learn from the adorers
around Christ in Bethlehem is the spirit of adoring more
and more. The adoring approach to Christ, urged by the
jubilant *Adeste*, should become a constant practice of our
lives and a permanent fruit of our Christmas celebration.

We have so many easy and glorious ways of adoring
Him. We can adore Him in the reverential postures of
our bodies, more or less copying the gestures of shepherds
and kings in front of their Saviour. We "glorify and bear
God in our bodies," as we genuflect in church and as we
kiss the feet of the Infant in the crib or the wounds of
the Man of sorrows on His cross. Sometimes our minds
are so dull and tired that we resemble the ox and the ass,
dumbly reverent in His presence. Yet we will to be near
Him, honoring Him.

We adore Him in so many of our prayers when we recite
the names of His divinity, "*Kyrie eleison* — Lord, have
mercy on us"; "Son of God, the world's Redeemer, have
mercy on us"; "My Lord and my God"; O divine Saviour,
Heart of God, have mercy on us. These phrases from our

Mass texts, our litanies, and our communion colloquies all lift up the spirit to honor the Word made flesh.

During the Mass the main moment for adoration occurs at the Consecration when He comes to our altar. Next in importance is the Communion when in His host form He comes into the house of our bodies and souls. Full verbal expression of our adoration comes at that early moment in the Mass when we join with priests and choir in the great prayer that begins with the angelic greeting to the shepherds:

> Glory to God in the highest;
> Peace and good will to men on earth!
> We praise Thee.
> We adore Thee.
> We give Thee glory.
> We give Thee thanks for Thy own great glory.
> O Lord God, King of Heaven, almighty God the Father.
> O Lord Jesus Christ, the only-begotten Son.
> O Lord God, the Lamb of God, the Son of the Father.
> Thou who dost away with the world's sins, have mercy on us.
> Thou who removest the world's sins, be gracious to our request.
> Thou who art enthroned at the right hand of the Father, do have mercy on us.
> For Thou art the only Holy One, the only Lord, the only Highest One,
> Christ Jesus, together with the Holy Spirit in the glory of God the Father. Amen.

This song of the angels is the Church's outburst of adoring love which breaks the patient silence of Advent. In this canticle of Bethlehem our needs and petitions are almost set aside. Instead we echo the heavenly choirs; we echo the praising phrases of the Our Father; we praise God in all three Persons; we invoke Christ's divine and redemptive titles; we confess to Him how great is His glory within the Blessed Trinity. It was fitting that this old Greek hymn should become one of the most loved parts of the Mass. First the Pope adopted it in his Christmas Mass; gradually bishops were permitted to use it in their Christmas Masses and newly ordained priests in their ordination Masses.[40] Now we all lift these golden invocations to Christ on Christmas Day and in many other Masses. Many a choir in Christendom tries to match the angel's full-throated beauty when they chant in Latin these praises to the newborn Saviour.

But the hours of the Mass are not our only chances for adoring love. We have opportunities to adore Him in visits to the Blessed Sacrament where the Christ in the crib is now the Christ within the host, truly and really the same God and our Emmanuel. He is in our neighborhood, just a little distance from us in our parish church, waiting for us to come like shepherds to visit our divine Neighbor. He is in those distant towns and cities through which we pass on our vacations; He is waiting for us in tabernacles, wondering if we will come like wise men from afar to visit Him. One of the nicest things about being a Catholic tourist is to find Christ everywhere and be able to visit Him at so many places along our route.

But chapels and cathedrals are not the only spots suited for adoration. All of us can gather together round the crib in our own homes whether it be mounted near the tree, or atop the piano, or in the children's bedroom. There we can join in family adoration, mother and father now taking the place of Mary and Joseph, and children taking the place of eager shepherds.

These shall be our answers to the Church's call to us, "Come, adore Him."

Mother of God by the manger, adoring your God in His little human body, teach us to adore Him, to glorify Him, and to love Him. Teach us your own better way of communing with the Son of God when He is present within us at Holy Communion.

7. THE GRACE OF A DIVINE CALL

CHOOSING THE CAST

God's activity in working out the details of the mystery of the birth of His Son has sometimes been compared to the recruiting, testing, and selecting of characters by a movie producer. God sought and trained the best characters for this major production initiated by His mercy.

He first selected His own divine Son for the central role of becoming man and in human form redeeming and

42

teaching men. The Letter to the Hebrews tells us of His response to the Father's call as He entered our world: Behold, I come, to do Thy will, O God.[41]

Next, God summoned Gabriel to be His willing messenger to the prospective mother of His Son. Playing his part in brilliant style, the angel of the Incarnation won Mary's consent to the divine invitation and the tremendous burden. Mary heeded the divine call: Behold, I am the handmaid of the Lord. Be it done to me, then, as you say.[42] She knew that God had chosen her in sheer condescension. He has looked on the littleness of His handmaid, she commented in the Magnificat.

Elizabeth's prayer for a child was answered in her old age when she was picked to play a supporting role as mother of the Baptist, Christ's forerunner, and as womanly confidant of Mary at the outset of her career.

Good St. Joseph was asked to be the virginal spouse of Mary, the human head of the Holy Family, the worker who supported them, and the guardian of the lives of mother and Son. He fulfilled His task to perfection.

A band of angels was deputed by the heavenly Producer to link heaven with earth in this drama of salvation by awakening the shepherds with a message and a shower of song. These herders, who believed in angels, were the first people of God to be called to know that the Saviour had been born and were invited to visit Him. These men received this beautiful reward for their hospitality in lending a shelter for the Infant.

The Magi, thoughtful and scholarly men, received their call through a new star. They knew the stars and the God of stars. They knew that only God could make a new star and have it point to a definite spot. Their vocation was not merely to believe in the meaning of the star, but to come on a long journey following the star, meet a strange setback at Jerusalem, find the star again, and perfect their faith and perseverance by adoring the Child, offering their precious gifts, discovering His Mother, and protecting His flight by their escape along another route.

Simeon and Anna had special parts in the drama as holy souls who recognized the Saviour and welcomed Him in God's temple. They became missionaries telling their friends of His coming.

The Holy Innocents also had a unique call: to be towns-men of Christ, born about His time, to be identified with His birth and birthplace, and to lay down their budding lives for their Saviour in whose imperiled cause they were included.

In all these vocations, God chose, and men responded. All true vocations begin with His good will to men. Some like Herod and the priests in Jerusalem who heard the news from the Magi did not respond to the chance. Both to those who co-operated with His plan and to those who would not receive His Son God had called: Come; come and see; come and adore; come and serve; come, do My will; come, be one with Christ; come, take some part in His birth and work. God's love called in every case. God's loving grace made possible the responses of Mary, Joseph, the angels, and the others. God in every instance left some-thing to the consent, the generosity, the free output of energy, and the spirit of sacrifice of the selected.

There were surprising individual differences in these calls from heaven. Yet God in His long foresight had prepared each one whom He called for special functions. Divine Providence always accommodates His gifts, His will, and His vocations to the personalities of each receiver. He called each in a special way: Mary He called in a private visit from an angel; Joseph in a dream; shepherds with great publicity; Magi by a stellar wonder. The ones who

bungled their part were the Hebrew scholars who knew of
Christ only through their prophetic books about His birth
in Bethlehem.

THE MASTER IS HERE AND IS ASKING FOR YOU[43]

These words of Martha to her sister Mary remind us
that Jesus Christ keeps coming into human lives. His
personal invitation to each human soul for some form of
loving service to Him and to His cause is like a continuance
of Christmas on earth. Christ issues a general call to all
men and special summons to selected souls. As some did
not accept Him in His time, some do not respond to His
sweet request now. Yet He wills all to come to the knowledge of the truth of His Father and of Himself and to be
saved by faith and love. He has called all of us to have
His faith, His baptism, His Church and no other, His grace,
His pardon, His promises, His Body and Blood, and His
Mother. He has called us all to bear His name, to be
Christians, Christ's men, Christ's followers, and members
of His Mystical Body. Most men and women have also
been called to come to Him at Bethlehem. For Bethlehem is the sacred symbol for home and the beginnings of
human life and love of children.

But Christ's invitations come to us in all the variety of
our characters, circumstances, and individual opportunities.
As His Father's providence has put us in our particular
historical setting, in this century, and in this country,
Christ adapts His will for us to these providential circumstances. He calls one young man to be a father, another
to be a priest, another to be a teaching brother, and
another to be a consecrated helper of his leaders. He calls
one young woman to be a contemplative nun, another a
nursing sister, another a teacher, a housekeeper; one to be

a mother with a big family, another to be a widow, another to be a virgin in the world caring for sick members of her family. Here He calls one to be a doctor or a scholar or a lawyer; there He calls another to be a merchant or a farmer or a journalist. Some He would have serve Him in health, others in illness; some by administering wealth for Him and His poor, others by bearing the aches of poverty. To some He gives singular aptitudes and unusual opportunities — which they and no others have — to aid in the salvation and happiness of certain particular people whom His providence moves into their sphere of influence. With wonderful wisdom Christ selects the cast of characters for every part and arranges the moments of contact between human lives for the sake of His Father's glory.

We discover, too, that the state and way of life to which He calls each of us is the happiest and best life that we could have. As life flows upward, our vocation proves to be deeper than we had expected. Instead of being a drop of grace, it turns out to be a whole river of graces; instead of being a single golden nugget of God's favor, it turns out to be a vast gold mine of unlimited opportunities for years of practicing virtues. As a production, it is a "sleeper." It seems to be like the Magi's trip to the crib. We heard His voice; we saw His star; we started to find Him. We may have expected a short journey, small hazards, not much sacrifice; and we did not know exactly what we would find at the end of the road. For all that, we trusted Christ. Until this day we have carried on, following the starry will of God as far as we see it, taking all the means which prudence and divine inspiration suggest, praying along the route, undiscouraged by delays and Herods and even the temporary disappearance of the star. Those who hold fast to their course will find what the wise men found: Jesus and Mary. It is enough.

Speak, Lord, Your Servant Listens[44]

What would God have me do? How would He prefer me to live? If I truly want His will, I will surely find it. He will not keep it secret. He may open up His will and welcome to me only step by step. But in His own good time He will use all divine ingenuity in making it known to me and then in giving me the help to do what He requests. He will be true. It is for me to seek His will and to open my spirit to His loving pursuit. Then He will find me wherever I am, whatever I am doing. He will turn my plans and other human plans into His plan. If I am willing and glad to hear Him, I will know His voice as surely as a bird identifies the call of its mate. For when God and I both wish that the will of God should be done in my life, it will be done. I can no more miss than Mary or Joseph, the shepherds or the Magi could have missed.

He who knows God's vocation for him, whether it be in home or office or factory or rectory or sickroom or cow barn — no matter — he now has to give himself wholly and determinedly to exploiting its full possibilities for the service of Christ and for perfecting the fine details to which the sweet insistent will of God invites the soul.

Those who persevere in following the heavenly voice will discover that the call to the crib is a prelude to the call to the throne where Mary's smiling eyes show us the glorious fruit of her blessed womb. Those who have sought the Master will find where He dwells eternally. They will hear Him calling at the hour of death: "Come, blessed of my Father, possess the kingdom prepared for you from the foundation of the earth."[45] Well done, good servant, enter into the joy of your Lord.[46]

Christ has come to us. We have come to Christ.

8. THE GRACE OF POVERTY OF SPIRIT

St. Paul recognized the poverty of Bethlehem as a token of God's love. He called the attention of his Corinthian converts to it: Brethren, you know the charity of our Lord Jesus Christ, how being rich He became poor for your sakes, that through His poverty you might be made rich.[47]

St. Francis fell in love with the poverty of Christ, his Sister Poverty. He congratulated some of his followers when they had to spend one Christmas Eve in a stable as Christ

had done. St. Catherine of Siena said of the homeless
Christ in his borrowed hut: "He descended into the stable
of our humanity that we might ascend to the temple of
His divinity." His love prompted Him to think this a fair
deal that the Prince of Heaven should become a pauper
on earth so that we poor beggars might become rich heirs
in His realm. God has acted to us as a Father who settles a
vast fortune on adopted children.

Painters have tended to glorify the Nativity scene instead
of retaining the original stark poverty of the gospel record.
The fact is that the Holy Family was poor and bore the
hardships of the poor. There was no room for them in the
inn, much less in any private home. No room meant no
rest after a hard trip, no warm food, no one to care for
the animal and luggage, no chance of giving special care
to the coming Child, no snug and scented cradle for the
little One, no pride in Mary's and Joseph's hearts that they
had given the very best to God at the dawn of redemption.
Discomfort, cold, little light, and slight protection from
the nightly changes of weather were part of life in their
borrowed hillside shelter. An animal refuge was the first
home on earth for God. It was an unfurnished spot, with
bare floors, soiled and crude, worse than quarters usually
allotted to slaves. Its chief furnishing was a feeding trough;
its supplies, some hay stored there for stormy weather.
This manger, a tacit loan from the shepherds, was His sign,
the visible birthmark of His spirit.

Mary who had been educated in the Temple could
have well imagined that His Father's splendid temple in
Jerusalem was the proper place for His birth. There the
finest linen and choicest bedding could have been His,
and His nursery would have been furnished with gold and
sandalwood, silks and purples. Fine baby blankets, glowing
fires, and the best medical care of the day could have been

His. Corps of Levites and their wives would have been His attendants. But His Father and her Son did not wish to be born among the rich.

Here they are away from their own home in Nazareth. Mary thought of the plans she had made for His birth in that sweet, clean home up North, of the clothing she had woven for Him, of the cradle Joseph had made, and of the economies they had been practicing to fit a spot for Him. She sympathized with Joseph's embarrassing disappointment that this cave was the best that he could provide for this glorious moment of the appearance of the King.

Their plans have gone astray because God had better plans. A Roman emperor's order has brought them here. Yet the poor Boy lying here is much greater than Caesar. They have had to labor, travel, and suffer for His birth under these conditions. Why did God not prevent or countermand Caesar's order? Caesar's son would be surrounded with luxuries. Costly presents, festive robes, blaring trumpets, the empire's best doctors and nurses, every form of pomp would have been his. But the King of Caesars did not want it that way for Himself. He did not even arrange that Mary and Joseph should have enough wealth to be able to make reservations long in advance, send ahead their own servants, and prepare a fine lodging for the coming God. God wanted Mary and Joseph for what they were and not for what they had. God had wealth in heaven; He came on earth to find the treasure of poverty.

This set of conditions is a deliberate preference of God. Omnipotent Providence could arrange all things just as He wished: the hour, the place, the furnishings, the dignity, the care were as much within divine choice as had been the selection of the Mother of God. God let the laws of

nature and the natural run of historical events bring
His Son to Bethlehem's cave.

THE GOD OF THE POOR

What is the plan of God in giving the privations of the
poor to His own Son, to His mother, and guardian father?

He chose it out of charity, says St. Paul: out of love
for Mary, for the poor, and for the sinful rich, but not out
of love for Himself.

First of all, poverty gave Mary some privacy to rejoice
over Him in the first hours of His life. A rich, well-known
lady would not have been alone with her divine Son.

Next, He would be like men in all things, save sin. But
most men are poor. He who loved all men would show
His love of the poor by coming very near to them. To
know our wants better, He would come under circumstances where the barest means of living would be His.
He would have to fly away to Egypt. He would learn a
trade, that of a carpenter. He would be at home among
fishermen. He would travel by foot. He would spend His
mature preaching years more homeless than a migratory
worker without a place that He could call His own. He
would die dispossessed of absolutely all earthly wealth.

He is the Saviour of the world, both of the poor and
the rich. Because He is ever so poor, the poor know that
in Him they can save their souls. They realize that His
is not a fair-weather religion or a faith for the elite, a hope
for the comfortable, a divine vocation for people of worldly
importance, a church for uptown and fashionable sub-
urbanites only. He is a God not unfamiliar with slums,
alleys, and crowded jungles in rundown districts.

He would also offer salvation to the rich. The rich, He

knew, need saving from their own riches and their worldly
desires to gain, retain, and increase their wealth even
at the cost of their souls and their opportunities for holiness. The poor, He knew, would need saving from the bad
example of the rich and from their dangerous desires to
own, control, and enjoy this world's goods in imitation
of the rich.

Christ has come as the Teacher of spiritual values to
men. Like a great teacher, He makes His first lesson a
most memorable one. It is a lesson in the unimportance
of wealth in the sight of God, a lesson in God's preference
for the inner heart of people. Christ knew what keeps so
many away from God. He saw the heart's clinging to the
things of earth. He knew why Herod would be so jealous
of Him, why Judas would betray Him, why the Pharisees
would kill Him, and why His Church would so often
suffer from robbers of her property and so seldom have
resources enough for her essential work. He knew how
men worried and lost their peace over income and how
concern for property left them no time for God and the
supernatural life of prayer and charity. Christ knew the
source of the worst forms of pride. He knew the grinding
injustice resulting from greed, the miseries of the poor, the
luxury and extravagance, the quarreling, and the wars of
conquest that would be due to wealth. He Himself is a
victim of Roman desire for wealth based on taxes. Taxes
demanded a census. The census sent Mary and Joseph far
from the simple comforts of home to a bare cave. Therefore, He underlines in the shivering stable this most important lesson of the freedom of the heart from this world's
goods.

He proclaims the special character of His kingdom this
night as a kingdom of the spirit. A poor King like this
who pitches His camp in a stall and has nothing but

straw stalks for His spears can have no intentions of worldly conquest.⁴⁸ His is unarmed power and powerful poverty for the conquest of souls.

THE POOR AT HEART

Let us be clear about what Christ is teaching from the crib. He is not recommending destitution or improvidence. But He is saying that the poor can be favored ones in the kingdom of God. He stresses it by calling hired shepherds to be His visitors; He bypasses the owners of the flocks. He picks the laborers, not the profiteers, for His courtiers. He is not teaching that no rich man can be saved; for prudence, justice, and charity all require that there be some abundance of wealth, well managed by someone for general human welfare. But He is teaching that the rich must be detached at heart from their riches and must avoid the evils to which possession so readily leads. He is not saying that riches in themselves are evil or that only the wicked possess them. But He is saying that they are usually dangerous, that they tend to keep the spirit away from God and open it to pride, injustice, cruelty, and indulgence. It will be hard for the rich and proud to be like Christ, the Man of the meek and humble heart. It is easier for the poor to be humble, because they are not much thought of and must bear the humiliation of being overlooked and of being considered as impersonal beings, mere hands, slaves, tools of the mighty and wealthy.

To imitate Christ, we do not have to rush out to stables to celebrate Christmas nor turn our maternity hospitals into old barns. But we must acquire Christ's respect for the poor and His practical interest in them. We must be willing for the love of Christ to give up some or all of our wealth if God should so wish it. We must guard our spirit against the hardness of the rich man's heart. We must bring ourselves to tell Christ of our readiness, for His glory, to serve Him in actual poverty, dependence, and some want. We can put ourselves to a test of sincerity by sharing some of our material wealth during this season with Christ or some cause dear to Christ, such as Catholic education. In this way we can prove that we forget self and have mastered our riches by joyous giving that youth may be trained, as the divine Child was trained, in the love of God and of the poor.

The grace of poverty of spirit is one of the deepest Christmas graces. For just as there are people who are young and others who, though old in body, are young at heart, so there are people who are poor and there are others, whether rich or poor, who are poor at heart, poor in spirit.

It is to these that Christ addressed His beatitude: "Blessed are the poor in spirit, for theirs is the kingdom of heaven."[49] For they exchange the riches of earth for the treasures of grace.

St. Joseph the Worker and Father of the Poor, pray for us that we may come close to Christ in His poverty and become contented with our lot.

9. THE GRACE OF A BIRTHDAY

A CHILD IS BORN TO US![50]

Some of the pleasure and grace of Christmas stems from
the fact that it is the birthday of someone who is very
dear to us. By this coming December 25 Christ is approach-
ing his two thousandth birthday. The memory of the
Church each year keeps this birthday with liturgical
splendor. For Christ belongs to the Church; Christ belongs to us. His beginnings are our beginnings in grace.
His birth is God's and Mary's gift to us. It is truly right
that we keep celebrating happy birthdays with Him.

55

With birthdays we link our ideas of new life, a new person to love in the home, added responsibilities, and fresh hopes. Births are times for announcements and greetings, for choosing a name for a new member of the family, for christening and sponsoring, and for plans for the future. The recurrence of the birthday is a day for parties, good wishes, gifts, and new resolutions for a fuller, better year.

The same associations and activities cluster around the most significant of all birthdays, that of Christ. Though He is eternally ancient and ever young in His divine life, in His human life He only once was the youngest baby on earth, nestling in His mother's arms. The eternal generation of the Son is unbeginning and unending and is eternally taking place. The novelty is His human birth. Christ has appeared as the new man of the new era of God on earth. He is the new Adam, come to undo all the death-dealing work of the old Adam. Everything about His coming and person was fresh and wonderful. Having more than natural human life in the soul and in the flesh, He came as the new Life of the world. He Himself was and remains God's altogether new gift to us. He came with a new offer of pardon from God on newer, easier terms. He came with new graces, sanctifying and actual. He came with new truths, new clearness, and bright mysteries to rejoice the soaring intellect. He came with new sparkling hopes, great promises and blessings, and a new inheritance. He came with God's latest gift of love. Beginning His reign on earth, He brought a new key to open the kingdom of heaven.

He inaugurated the new age of the Incarnation. All else is dated as before or since His birth, for He is the pivot of all history. With Him begins the New Testament and the cycle of the years of the Lord, "A.D." For long years, as historians know from many documents, His birthday in many regions was also New Year's Day, for it seemed fitting that all new things should begin with Christ's birth.

The newborn King came with a new law, the law of charity and peace, to replace the old cold law of justice and anxiety. The very accent of God's commandments in dealing with men now turns from the control of sinners and the mastery of His servants to the tender friendship of God with His beloved friends. God's Son came to set up a new agreement between God and men. This new covenant brought in a whole new religion, ending both the Hebrew religion and the best in paganism. For the new High Priest has come from heaven, ordained by God to offer a new sacrifice and be the new Victim immolated in this spotless worship to God. He brought, then, not only a new faith with its new truths and a new code with its high morality of charity and chastity, but also a new cult with a new sacrifice, the Mass, new ministers, and new sacraments. He brings a new conception of marriage as a copy of His deathless espousal with His Church.

He brings His Church with Him as one of His birthday gifts to us; for to Him this celebration is more a time for giving to us than for receiving from us. His birth, says St. Leo I,[51] is the birthday of the Church and of the Mystical Body, as well as of His physical body. A new religious society, a fellowship, and organization for our social spiritual life began this day. At His birth the divine seed of His Church was sown; His later life and later history unfold the seed; heaven is its endless harvest in the Church triumphant.

CELEBRATING WITH CHRIST

If we would have a deep Christmas spirit, we must spend this birthday with Christ. Today is His party. He

invites us to be His guests at His feast. He asks us only
to come, as He asked the shepherds and Magi. If we also
bring gifts, He will be very glad, particularly if they be
gifts of the spirit. But He will be content if we do but
come to Him; time will do the rest if only we are near
Him. He will ask us to sing at His party, as He asked
the angels to fill the skies with melody for Him. He will
offer us His own gifts of grace and gladness and the Food
of the sons of God. He may invite us even to come very
close to Him and serve Him, as He requested Joseph and
Mary to do. But this is His day. We do whatever will
please Him. We do whatever He asks. We take His joy
and give Him ours.

Even our feasting at home with family and friends
should be a party in His honor and a toast to His
memory. For He is the Heart of Christmas. We celebrate
first of all for His sake. As groups of politicians gather in
many cities on Jefferson's or Lincoln's birthday, so Christians gather with other Christians on December 25 to
feast in memory of the birth of their King and God.

Because He was a little Child, we remember today to
be specially kind to children. They are the latest copies
of the new life of Christ. Whatever we do to one of
these little children, we do to Him.[52] We owe it to
Christ to make our children happy at Christmas and to
bring them close to the Christ who gave them Christmas.

That Christ Be Born in Your Hearts

We are little children of whom the Church is in labor
until Christ be born and formed in us. Our true birthday
in Christ was the day of our baptism. Christmas is somewhat a souvenir of our christening when we received the
new life of Christ in our souls. This day of Christ's begin-

nings prompts us, then, to start anew in the Christian life and begin again with youthful vigor to proceed in the Christian ascent to perfect companionship with Christ. While there is life in us, there are fit moments for a renewal of grace and livelier vigor in our graced activity. Faith can be refreshed; hope can be revived; love of God can be revitalized; innocence can be restored to us; our spiritual energy can be regenerated; and new resolutions can be offered as birthday favors for Christ. The truths of Christ are just as good news as they ever were. Hearing these truths, we not only feel bright wonder and sing new canticles to the Lord, but also determine anew to live for the Lord, to live like Christ, and to share with Christ in His life of grace. Newly liberated from the old yoke of sin, on this new birthday of Christ we start again with fresh supplies of Christ's grace, with new opportunities for virtue, with new desire to conquer the old enslaved man and put on the new free man of the dawning age of the Incarnation.[53]

Christ our Lord, may Your birthday be happy not merely because of the candles that we light in Your honor and the cup that we drink in Your name. May its happiness come from You and glow in the love to which You give birth in our hearts. Child of God's love, teach us children of God to love in deed and in truth.

10. THE GRACE OF A GIVING HEART

THEY OFFERED HIM GIFTS

Everyone connected with the coming of Christ had a generous heart.

God so loved the world that He gave His only-begotten Son.[54] The Son was given to us.

God the Son gave Himself as our fellow man, our companion, and our Redeemer. The Epistle of the first Christmas Mass reminds us of this gift of divine grace and the redemptive cleansing wrought by Christ.[55]

God the Holy Spirit, the very Gift within the Godhead, devised the miracles of the Incarnation and the Virgin Birth.

Mary gave her consent, her love, her life, her flesh and blood, her career, and her care to give us Christ our Redeemer. Her Child is born as a gift for us.

Joseph gave all that he could to guard Him and all that He could earn to support the Christ Child.

The angels gave their songs and services as messengers to us.

The shepherds came with their wonder and gave their praises as they spread the word among their people.

The wise men came with mystic gifts to adore Him. Whatever the hidden symbolism of these gifts may be, their vivid meaning of homage, faith, and loving offering of the best of their home countries is plain.

Simeon and Anna gave jubilant thanks that He had come to bless their old age.

The little Innocents gave their lives for Him.

All who were near Christ caught that spirit of gift-giving. Words and praises, wondering gasps and shining promises were not enough. They must do all they can. They must serve and give, for all the world understands the language of gifts as the language of sincere friendship.

The spirit of love and the spirit of giving go together. The New Testament, the rule of God's love, is to be also the era of exchange of gifts between God and men. The angels announced Christ's policy of giving: giving glory to God, giving all that pertains to peace among men. That night began the unending chain of the gifts of divinity and of redemption. The series of divine gifts shall never end, for it will go on forever in the glories of heaven. The newborn Child is a Fountain of gifts. His charity has begotten the whole world-wide custom of Christmas presents. His desire to give is so strong that He urged us to ask in His name, for His glory, and it would be given to us.

If we ask why He gives to us and wills to give more, the answer cannot be that we are so wonderful, so full of merits, so deserving of a gift of His. He is perfectly free in dealing with us and owes us nothing. His inner nature as divine love is the secret of His desire to give. His generosity is the beginning of all the good things that are ours at Christmas. God's liberality, Jesus' kindness, and Mary's charity saved the world. In the infinite gladness of His love for man, God loves to give His finest and to share His all with us. Therefore, He gave us His Son and intends to give us Himself in heaven. For God, the joy of life is the joy of giving.

Give Us This Day

Knowing that Christ loves to give to us and that indeed we would not even wish to give to Him unless He first gave us His grace, we realize that we can make Him happy on Christmas Day by asking much of Him. We beg that He would turn our unconverted hearts from the miserliness of old Scrooge into the giving hearts of true Christians. We ask Him for our daily bread, for His pardon, and for His protection against all evils, as He has instructed us to plead in the Our Father. We ask for His peace in our lives. We ask for the dearest grace of all, His charity to God and to all men. We ask for His spirit of forgiveness to those who have offended us. We ask Him again for true gratitude to Him and His Mother for what they have done for us in the first and all past Christmases. We ask for gracious courtesy in accepting gifts from others so that our very manner of receiving may delight the givers the more. We ask for a lasting personal intimacy with

Christ in the Blessed Sacrament and a never failing growth in His love.

Give us, dear Christ, all this and whatever else You wish. Give us, as Your Church begs, the gift of immortal loving vision of our Redeemer.[56]

Accept, O Lord, These Holy Gifts, Presents, and Sacrifices

This line of the Canon of the Mass voices our desire to give to Christ some return for His bounty to us. We are poor, yet would like to give some wonderful gift to God and something that would match His excellence. Fortunately, His goodness has made it possible for us to offer a perfect gift to Him. For the Christ, whom God gave us can be offered to God in the loving sacrifice of His human nature in the Mass. We must tender this gift with as perfect hearts and as generous dispositions as we can command by good preparation for Christmas Mass and Communion.

But this gift of the Mass is not our only possible gift. We can offer our service to Him by uniting our wills with His holy will, by giving loving obedience to His laws, by loving all that He loves, by giving to His poor brethren, and by showing Him that unmistakable sign of love for Him: "By this shall all men know that you are My disciples, if you have love one for another." Love in deed and in work removes all sham and superficiality from our efforts to give to Christ.

We give to others according to our capacity as well as according to their needs, but for His sake. We are anxious not merely to give enough in the name of Christ, but even more: to be giving with a deep enough spirit, motive, and perfection of manner. Our gifts may be greetings, smiles, or prayers for others; they may be presents; or neighborly good turns and festivities planned for others; or surrender of our prejudices and grudges and rights. But all are inspired by Christ's giving and flow from a desire to copy Christ's and Mary's generous spirit. If we are giftless to our fellow men, we are empty-handed when we appear before the crib and before the altar rail. And that will never do. What we give to our brethren, we give to Him. What we give is given back to us in divine ways,[57] for God never lets Himself be outdone in generosity. Our loving gifts on earth shall return in heaven as permanent souvenirs of our Christmas heart. The orphan, refugee, widow, or missionary whom we befriended stands before God's throne more splendid than the fabulous gifts of Melchior, Gaspar, and Balthasar gleamed before the eyes of the Infant in the manger.

11. THE GRACE OF LIGHT

I Am the Light of the World

The swaddling clothes and the manger are the primary signs connected with the humanity of God become an infant. Light is the primary sign pointing to the divinity of this human Child.

Light sparkles in many scriptural references to Christ and in many of the liturgical texts of Christmas. The prophetic promise that a mighty light would shine upon us has come true. Zachary foresaw Him as the rising sun who would shine on all who sit in ancient darkness. The brightness of God shines round the shepherds, startling them into a state of fear. The band of angels gleams in the skies like golden birds whirling among the points of the stars. The light silvers the Judean hills and adorns them with its sequined dew. The new star of the divine King hangs like a jeweled brooch on the dark gown of the heavens. In the cave, the Light of the world glows from the face of the divine Child and is showered upon every face and corner.[58] Before Christ's cradle days are ended, Simeon will foresee Him as the light of revelation to the gentiles, not reserved to the Jews. He who had commanded that light be made has himself come in light.

Later in life Christ would more than once say that he was the Light of the world. St. John would proclaim the Word as the Life of the world, and as the Light shining in darkness, as the Light to whom the Baptist gave witness, as the true Light that enlightens every man in the world, as the Glory of the Only-begotten of the Father seen on earth.

Christians have made every light at this season a memory of and a tribute to the Light of the world. We wed words about light to clear music in our songs of the holy night. We brighten our homes with decorations. We set a candle within the Christmas wreath. We turn mere trees into fairylands of light and set a gleaming star in their crowns. We must have candles on our Christmas tables and the sheen of lamps in our churches. For this is more than a birthday; this is the feast of the divine light.

Christ the Light is one of His loveliest names, and He well deserves it. He is the Light because He is the Word of God, generated by the intellectual activity of His Father within the nature of God. He is the Wisdom of His Father expressed in a second divine Person. He is

the imaged Splendor of His Father's infinite knowledge.
He is the Truth and the Source of all truth. The Church
in the great creed of the Mass refers to Him as God from
God, Light from Light, true God from true God.

Hail, Holy Light!

He is, moreover, the divinely sent Teacher to instruct all
men in the things pertaining to God. He is the Light who
is to uncover the secrets of heaven for us and to pierce the
inky darkness of our ignorance, blindness, and error. His
light cannot be extinguished. No prejudice can imprison
Him; no opposition can limit Him. No man can reveal
truth to Him, for it is all His by divine right and divine
gift. He is the Light itself, a pure self-luminous light, an
original sun, the very first cause of all knowledge. He does
not reflect light like a planet or a mirror. He needs no
light. He seeks no light from men. He is the Light and
gives light to others. For this He came into the world that
men might know Him and His Father and that men might
follow Him out of dead and wicked darkness into the ways
of living light.

One of the occasions on which our Lord called Himself
the Light of the world was during the feast of Tabernacles
at Jerusalem when the Hebrews commemorated the pillar
of fire which had led them by night on their way out of
dark Egypt into the promised land.[59] Christ made that
pillar of light leading His people into a symbol of His own
function for all men. He saw the brilliantly lit temple as
a dim picture of His own interior spiritual light as Wisdom
of God and Teacher of truth.

Probably no created symbol could better express for us
this divinity of Christ and this teaching function of His
humanity. Light makes the unseen visible to the senses

and, by their help, to the intellect. When things are illuminated, we cry: Now I see. Light guides us and shows the way; by day and night it is the sailor's and the traveler's and the searcher's main aid on his course. Light is a symbol of life; for it is a cause of growth, it quickens health, it accompanies the budding and ripening of most organisms. Light warms and comforts, as our sun-loving age knows well. Light, because it purifies and cleanses, is a symbol of innocence and holiness and of the grace that expels evil. Light so imponderable and powerful, coming to earth by the sheer bounty of heaven, and swiftly spreading everywhere, makes us think of the immaterial mighty nature of God, gratuitously blessing us and uncontained in His dominion over the whole world. Light's colors and manifold effects beautify people and objects. Light gladdens the heart. Light gives security to the lonely and unprotected. Light drives evil into hiding. Light even seems to give some companionship; for men, when alone, will start a fire in the hearth to let it substitute for missing friends. Light also glorifies and attends the victor on his triumphal march.

What light is to our bodily, mental, and social life, Christ is to all men and especially to his followers whom He has called the children of light. Christ is our Truth; Christ is our Guide; Christ is our Life of the spirit; Christ is our heaven-sent God; Christ is our Beauty; Christ is our Safety; Christ is our Guest; Christ is our Victor. We are convinced, as the Magi were, that He is the Star who has revealed God to us in His person and the truths of God in His teachings. We are so glad and so thankful that God gave us the favor of finding Christ and joining the glorious company of those who believe in Him. For our acceptance of Christ's revelation no less than the revelation itself is a sheer gift of God to us. The true God did not let the god of this world blind us to the light of the gospel of the glory of Christ, but He who commanded light to shine out of darkness has shone in our hearts and irradiated our minds with the knowledge of that glory of God which shines on the face of Jesus Christ.[60]

YOU ARE THE LIGHT OF THE WORLD!

It has pleased the Star to call us into the kingdom of His light. He has told us plainly what religious truth is. Now that He has disappeared from the world, He has left His Church as His star to guide us to Him. Over and above the public ways of revelation and of the Church's teaching, Christ the Truth moves us by individual inspirations of grace, for instance, to think of God, to make some good resolution, or to begin some prudent good work. In whatever way His light comes into our lives, we children of the light joyfully welcome it. Even when the light shines in our consciences and demands some sacrifice of self-will, we still give thanks for the light. For we are determined to do as He ordered us: to walk in His light.

It has pleased the great original Light to call us also lights for the world. We are lanterns set afire by His brightness; we are set on high hills where men can see Christ's light reflected in our lives. We pray that we may shine worthily for His sake and teach by word and example nothing that is against His truth.

We pray that God will send His Son's light into the lives of those who do not yet see it and even into the minds of those who are afraid of the truth or hate it.

We pray, too, that the glory of His light will shine this Christmas upon souls dear to us who have been yearning in purgatory for the coming of His glorious star.

For ourselves we ask the grace ever to love the whole

truth and ever to be proudly loyal to its demands. We beg for more light. We beg to march with the Magi wherever the light leads, as far as Bethlehem, as far as Calvary, as far as heaven. We beg with the Church praying for us in her Masses on December 25 and January 6: that we may be candles that will lead men to Christ, that His light may shine in our works so that glorious deeds may glorify Christ,[61] and that some day we may exchange the quiet light of faith for the beating light of the vision of God in paradise.[62] In Your light we shall see You, the Light. Then, lead us by Your bright paths until we reach that light in which You dwell.[63]

If the Face in the crib is so bright, what must be the Face on the throne!

12. THE GRACE OF THE SHADOW

His Own Received Him Not

The joy of Christ began as He lay folded in Mary's arms. The passion of Christ began that same night as He lay in the shed.

The lantern hung high by Joseph lighted up His baby features. But where there is light on earth, there is usually shadow as well. The shadow of a coming cross lay in dark streaks across the walls and floors of the cattle stall that midnight.

His first cry as His human lungs expanded in our atmosphere gave the signal for the beginning of His suf-

ferings. His intelligence, unlike that of other human
infants, knew by His infused knowledge the full sig-
nificance of the events and their relation to His future
life. The very moment that He came He knew He had
come for suffering: You did not wish sacrifices and offer-
ings. But you fitted me a body. And I said, Behold, I
come, my God, prepared to do Thy will.[64] He knew that He
was High Priest and Victim. His obedient, loving offering
of Himself, of His pain of body, and of anguish of spirit
began that night.

He felt the wood of the manger; it sent His mind leaping
to the wood of the cross. He felt the swaddling clothes
about Him; it told Him of the seamless robe of Mary of
which they would strip Him and of the shroud that would
be wound round His corpse. He had come from heaven
where there was no shadow, evil, or pain. Mary had given
Him a body in which to share human pain, a soul in which
to bear human shame and agony. She had given Him flesh
to be torn, blood to be shed, heart to be pierced, face to
be bruised, hands and feet to be nailed. As she caressed
Him, His mind raced ahead to the hot lashes of Good
Friday.

His very name, Jesus, was an ominous name. For this is
a saviour's name. Saviours must pay a great ransom of personal toil and compassion for the saved. Saviours seal
a new covenant with God; and where there is a covenant,
there must be blood-letting and the death of the giver so
that the heirs may receive his estate.[65] He knew all this.
He volunteered for it all. He was glad to be man in order
to begin His sufferings for men.

The cheap accommodations of this borrowed substitute
for a home also spoke of the hardships that would char-
acterize His life.

The notable absence of some classes of attendants foreshadowed the conflicts of His coming days. None of the mighty and wealthy of earth are near Him or care to come to Him. No Roman rulers, no Jewish priests, no Greek sages, no artists from Ephesus, no merchants from Antioch, no civil or military officials are here. The few locally important people who learn of Him do not come or send soldiers to kill Him. His circumcision began the process of the shedding of His blood. His flight into Egypt began the long manhunt for His life. Simeon's frank prophecy that He was a sign of contradiction and the occasion of the sword to be thrust into His mother's spirit sums up the shadows that surrounded the infant Christ.

For us the joy, for Him the pain. He wanted it that way all His life.

The Sign of Contradiction

In a world full of sin, fond of sin, and cursed by its own sin, an innocent and all-holy Redeemer could have had no other course than a long war between Himself and all the forces of evil. Evil, we say, is the lack of due good; moral evil is the privation of due good in the choices of the will, the deliberate absence of virtue in the character, the turning away of the inner man from His allegiance to God. Evil we call a shadow, a wound, and a gap in required being, life, or goodness. When God came to fill up what was missing, to throw light on the dark shadowed places, to heal the wounds, to complete our being, and to enrich us with good divine life, God Himself must meet the fierce forces of evil in their last stand against the conquering mercy of the Word made flesh. It could not be easy to be the Redeemer of a world so badly infected with sin. This new King came with a challenge to selfishness. Perhaps better than he realized, Herod spoke and acted for the forces of evil when he decided to meet the divine Challenger at the very outset of His life. He and they would have none of this Christ. Therefore, he made war on the Child and children.

Simeon put it very well when He saw in the face of the Babe presented in the Temple on the day of Mary's ritual purification that He was a sign of contradiction, a sign set up by God for the salvation and the fall of many. Men must henceforth be divided into two parties. Are they for Christ or against Christ? What do they think of Christ? Is He God or not? Is He Saviour or not? Is He King or not? Will they prefer Christ or themselves? Will they meet His challenge and follow Him; or refuse His challenge and go away from Him, sadder than the rich young man? Will they choose Him and all He stands for, including His humility and His cross; or will they choose self and Satan, including his pride and his torments? Those who hate the light will hate His revelation and prefer the cunning knowledge of Lucifer. Those who love themselves will not be able to bear the white fire of His holy love. Those who will not shake off their earthly desires will not have the least interest in a King with heavenly treasures as His gifts.

Years later Christ would say of Himself that He had come to bring the sword. He knew as a Child that the seven swords must pierce into His mother for her love and service of Him; and this was a great sorrow to Him even as an infant. His compassion for her began especially when she must fly away with Him from the murderous design of Herod. Yet He knew that these shadows athwart her joy were great graces for her, great gifts of God, coins that would purchase great rewards for her in heaven, sacrifices that would inspire glorious martyrs among His future followers.

He knew, too, that He was bringing a sword into many lives. Many a convert must choose Him instead of family, family affection, and family inheritance. The choice might cause tragic misunderstanding — as that between Edith Stein and her Jewish mother who was ever asking, "Why did He have to make Himself God?"[66] Many a martyr must be separated from all loved ones for His sake. Many a priest, nun, and brother must find the love of Christ cutting keenly into his and her human love, demanding preference of Jesus Christ to all else on earth. His law, like a sword, would keep lovers apart — to their human anguish but to their eternal gain. His justice, like a sword, would bar the way to invasion of the property, honor, and lives of other men. His code of marriage would cleave like a sword, often bringing sacrifice to those who would stand by His standard of chastity and of procreation. Yes, He knew that He was bringing shadows into many lives. But He had God's sight to know that the shadows would later leap into the triumphant light of heaven.

SACRIFICIAL GIFTS

The shadows of sin have no gleams of glory. The shadows of love of the Redeemer gleam with bits of the future glory of paradise. Sometimes in this life we come to learn that the sufferings of body and of spirit borne for Christ were among the most precious experiences of our lives. This may be of some comfort to those who on Christmas Day languish in hospitals, lie expecting death and the coming of the rewarding Judge, or who are far from home in military stations, or repent in prison for their misdeeds, or slouch along Skid Row, yearning to return to Christ but finding the road back so very slow and steep.

It is fitting that all of us compassionate Christ in His Christmas passion. It is urgent that we compassionate Christ in His members who suffer at Christmas. Christ the fugitive from Bethlehem is still fleeing from Herods in Communist lands. It is right to admit that He may demand heroism of us in living for Him. It is even possible to add to the joy of our Christmas by offering our sufferings to Him, even as Mary and Joseph offered the pain of their hearts and as the wise men offered their fears of treachery from Herod.

Christ the Redeemer, if we would help You in Your saving tasks, we, too, must step into the shadow of the cross and let You set the cross upon our shoulder. If we imitate Your infant cries by crying, ask Your Mother to comfort us as she comforted You. But do not lift the cross from us until You choose to do so. For we need both the light and the shadow of Bethlehem.

13. THE GRACE OF PEACE

THE PRINCE OF PEACE

The title, Prince of Peace, is one of Christ's fairest names. Given to Him by the prophet Isaias,[67] it was caught up by the angels when they sang of His mission to men: Peace on earth to men. When this King of peace came during the Augustan temporal peace, He revealed His peace policy in the signs of the infant smile, the swaddling clothes, and soft starlight. He is full of power and authority, yet comes frail and unarmed to declare His reliance on love and the spirit as His means of winning human hearts. Con-

77

scious of His peace mission, He speaks of peace the night before He dies. Triumphant on Easter Day, He greets His many heartsick friends with His famous words: "Peace be with you." "Peace; it is I; fear not."

The example of Christ is a long lesson in peace. The very manner of His coming is gentle, unpretentious, peace-loving. He comes from His Father with a spontaneous offer of pardon, foregoing divine justice and renewing man's friendship with God. His way in the crib, on the roads, and upon the cross shows His uninterrupted attention to the cause of peace. He makes every effort to win men. He is most courteous and approachable. He shows unlimited willingness to help. He trusts men, even those whom He foresees will desert Him. He obeys authority. He is calm, meek, untouched with bitterness even in facing opposition and bearing suffering. He continues unruffled in every situation. Dignity and kindness shine in every action from cradle to grave. His battles were only against the well-known foes of peace: sin, unbelief, insincerity, disordered human desires, injustice to anyone. His anger touched only hypocrites and sacrilegious profiteers in His Father's temple.

His words taught peace. His doctrines mean to end the very causes of disorder and to bring in the virtues that promote calm and contented relations among men. By spiritual error and bad will men rip apart the order within their own human natures, rend the order that should stand between their lives and God's will, and make enemies of their fellow men. Christ would set up good order by turning men to the primary search for the kingdom of God. With rectification of the will established, other order will follow. His rules on justice, on human kindness, on moderation of earthly desires, on the golden rule of conduct, and on meekness and chastity would keep out of men's lives all the sources of conflict, anxiety, fear, and hatred.

His work on earth, begun this night in the cave, merits for Him the name, Prince of Peace. Christ is our peace, its cause and its price. By His offering of Himself to come to earth for us, He begins the new world of grace. By His sacrifice He will reconcile God and men, reunite heaven and earth, remove the roots of disorder in self-will, and divinely help men to forgive each other, to bear with one another, to assist one another, and to persevere in true brotherhood. He will give Himself in Holy Communion as the bond of peace between His brethren. He will always pray before His Father in heaven for our peace. He will go to all lengths to make us love one another as He has loved us. In the kingdom of His truth, peace, and love all men of good will can enjoy firm friendship. For the Prince of Peace is the God of justice and charity.

Perhaps the strongest sign of His peace is His sleeping in the gentle arms of His mother. Is this a Warrior, Leader of a punitive expedition, a Judge, an Avenger? He sleeps in heavenly peace on that holy, silent night. No power of evil stirs to disturb this peace, "So hallowed and so gracious is the time."[68]

Christ's Peace Surpassing All Understanding

Peace in the heart of each Christian and peace among men is the very glory of Christ. The more the peace, the greater His glory.

His peace is unlike any other. It is given by Christ, modeled by Christ, taught by Christ, guided by Christ, merited by Christ, practiced by Christ, centered on Christ. Like any true peace, His is a peace marked by universal justice in all areas of rights and by contentment in the areas of order set up by the practice of justice. Men at peace are at peace with God, with themselves, and with all their fellows in the many social relationships of life.

But His peace is better than any other. For it is more complete, more serene, more enduring, and prophetic of the eternal peace of heaven. Christ's peace is meant to be a total peace, for all spheres of action and for all men, individually and socially. Christ's peace is a gladder peace, for it is founded on interior gifts of God and on the solid practice of great Christian virtues. Christ's peace is more enduring, for it has powerful divine helps to keep it lasting in our desires, intentions, and efforts. Christ's peace on earth is the prologue to our eternal peace in company with God, Mary, the angels, and saints. An order totally Christian on earth does the will of Christ on earth as it is done in heaven. Order is said to be heaven's first law because God's will reigns there in perfect love and, therefore, in perfect order of all under God.

One of the most beautiful images of Christ represents Him as Prince of Peace standing, looking down upon and across this world, presiding over divine order on earth, and blessing the cause of peace in the hearts of men of good will.

BLESSED ARE THE PEACEMAKERS!

The angels had hinted that men of bad will could not participate in the peace of God brought by the sweet Cause of our peace. Its blessings were offered them, as salvation is universally offered; but they are among those who do not receive Christ and do not want His peace. It reminds us that we must be willing to turn to Christ for our peace and follow the way of Christ in the gaining of peace.

Years later the Prince of Peace would in many ways urge His followers to be men of peace and promoters of peace.

One of the high points in His preaching of peace comes in the Sermon of the Mount when He utters His special blessing on peacemakers.[69] He begins by telling us not to be worriers and not to be troublemakers. He is telling us to love peace, to win it for ourselves, and to spread it to others. He is telling us to be fair to all in all matters; He is telling us to love all; He is telling us to be selfless; He is telling us to check all our passions, which disturb our own natures and disturb calm, constructive dealings with other men. He is telling us to trust God, to refrain from evil, to do things in the right, prudent way, and to use all due natural and supernatural means of setting up and keeping peace among all whom we can influence. The Christian peacemaker is a diplomat whose weapons are a love of God and a love of men and a sincere unwavering desire for true peace, no matter how much it may cost.

At the very least, we can all serve the Prince of peace by praying for the reign of His peace among men. This is perhaps the first and the last and the most effective measure that anyone can take. To him who prays well for peace, the steps in peacemaking will become clear.

Mary, Queen of Peace, in utter peace clasping the Prince of Peace, pray for us that we may be worthy of this promised peace of your Son.

Prince of Peace, lead us all into the kingdom of Your peace. Lead us peacefully along Your peaceful ways. Give peace to our families, our country, and Your Church in our times.

Divine Peacemaker, give us the courage and love to be peacemakers for Your sake.

Lamb of God, who takest away the sins of the world, give us Your peace,[70] that peace which the world cannot give, that peace which outruns all our understanding, the peace of Christ in the kingdom of Christ.

14. THE GRACE OF JOY

Joy tumbles like a merry waterfall from the hills of Bethlehem. One feels it rising within the buoyant greetings, praises, and predictions of Gabriel at the Annunciation. The coming of Christ breaks the good news to the world, that evangel or wonderful message which the gospel writers, evangelists, recorded. An angel, perhaps it was Gabriel, had swooped into the commonplace, rugged, and somber lives of the watchers of sheep, startling them

82

with a glad message: Behold I bring you tidings of great joy, for today is born to you a Saviour who is Christ the Lord.[71] Thereupon angels peopled the midnight skies, while their voices turned Christmas forever into a festival of song: "Gloria in Excelsis Deo."

Indeed, this was grand news to evoke the joy of the shepherds' souls. God, the Saviour, has come. He has come in person, not by messenger or prophets, not by photograph, telephone, or televised appearance. He has come in the flesh and now lies nearby in swaddling clothes. He has come to them. He has come today. He has come with mercy to save and with love to change the world into a place where God's glory and human peace can flourish.

The reporters of the good news also relate that the wise men rejoiced with exceedingly great joy when their guiding star shone again.[72] We can imagine their even greater joy when they found the Child with Mary His Mother. We are also told of the joy of Anna and Simeon in the Temple. We are left to guess at the happiness in the hearts of Christ, His Mother, and St. Joseph. Many think that angel songs were the original outburst of gladness that re-echoes down the centuries in our much loved Christmas hymns and carols. But others believe that it was the Virgin Mother's lullaby to her Child which set the angels singing. Her voice of delight is faintly heard accompanying every note of Christmas music.

Joy is part of the authentic spirit of the New Testament. The Advent liturgy has been promising joy to those who eagerly prepare for Christ. Zachariah's prophecy has been on the Church's lips: Rejoice, daughter of Sion. Behold, thy King cometh, the Holy One, the Saviour.[73] Now that His coming has renewed this third joyful mystery of the Rosary, the festive mood of the Church flowers like a lover's delight in the company of her beloved. Yearning is absorbed in urgent gladness: "Let the heavens be glad and the earth leap with joy, for He has come!"[74]

The Church is right. We should be glad for Christ's sake and for our own. He has come! God is with us. Redemption has begun. The old winter of sin is dying. The springtime of redemption has begun. Mary's bud is in blossom. The King is at hand. His light is shining in the East. The footfall of the Child can be heard in the hay, beating the rhythm of the angelic *Gloria*.

Christian joy is a gift of God to the spirit of man. It is a divine grace in our minds and wills that springs from belief in Christ's goodness and love as its principle, that is based on spiritual motives, and that attains spiritual objects known by faith. Sometimes it is called spiritual consolation. Sometimes it overflows into the sensible emotions and finds expression in the bright smile, soaring song, glad greetings, and festive family fun. Such joy can be long lasting in the soul. It is compatible with bodily suffering and even with a somewhat phlegmatic disposition that does not easily respond to the spirit's appreciation of spiritual good. Spiritual joy surpasses desire; for it has come to rest, delighted at the divine good within its grasp. It is above hope, for it has or all but has the beloved good as its own. It adorns the soul as health and laughter adorn the comely face, for it perfects love with conscious possession of its good. But its emotional elements may change, flicker, fade, and brighten again. God sometimes treats the soul as the morning sun treats the waters of a curving river. At dawn the river is a pageant of beauty, infinitely lovelier than autumn woods. But as the light grows brighter, the unique bloom vanishes; yet the light is there, and the river is there. So God still shines on the river of our lives, even when the radiant hues of His joy escape the surface of our existence.

The motives of our Christmas joy are multiple and mighty. There is joy in knowing that God has so loved the world that He sent His only-begotten Son and that the goodness and kindness of God our Saviour has appeared. There is the joy of a people when their glorious King has come to His own. There is the infinite loveliness of His surprising coming in the winsome weakness of a Child. There is the happiness of a birthday party with Mary's Boy, our Brother. There is our joy of mind in mystery and miracle in the Incarnation. There is the joy of seeing His glad Mother, of hearing the angelic concert, of witnessing Christ's first victories as Jewish shepherds and Gentile sages come to His feet.

There is joy for our own sakes, too, in knowing that we are dear to God, in receiving His great gifts so personally and graciously and imaginatively bestowed on us. There is the joy of knowing that the mighty Saviour will meet our spirit's tremendous needs for pardon, for truth, for help, for heaven. Our joy becomes even fuller when we realize that Christ gladdens all children by whom He is known and loved, as well as all homes in which He is welcomed and honored.

Who but God could bring so new, so deep, so sweet, so strong a joy to this worn, burdened, and sorrowing world? God and His Son and His Mother are the causes of our joy. May they be thanked as they deserve.

Come Joyfully, All Ye Faithful!

Crashaw's enthusiastic lines in the full chorus of his *Nativity* are one of the many responses of the human heart to the swelling grace of Christ's joy in us:

Welcome, all wonders in one sight!
  Eternity shut in a span.
Summer in winter. Day in night.
  Heaven in earth, and God in man.
Great little one! whose all-embracing birth
Lifts earth to heaven, stoops heav'n to earth.

God provides for our need of happiness in this world.
He cares for this human need often without our preparation and deserts. He moves majestically and unexpectedly
into our lives, bringing us objects and occasions of joy.
He provides generously for our need of the tonic of happiness at the Christmas season. We must prepare ourselves
for the divine gifts of joy. We must cherish the gift when
it comes. We must remember the love with which God
presents these favors. We must rejoice in the promises of
Christ to us. We must seek our joy in possessing lasting
heavenly goods and the image of such goods on earth. We
must be glad to be on God's side in both sunny and stormy
weather of the spirit. We must be glad, too, that God has
been so good to others besides ourselves and rejoice with
their successes for God. We must offer our joy to God for
His glory on earth. We must offer our joy to Christ as a
tribute to His gracious power to make His followers
happy.

We must measure up to our vocation, like that of
the shepherds and Mary, to spread our joy to others,
bearing to others the good news of the arrival of the gifts
of Christ. We must pray that others receive God's joy:
May the God of hope fill them with all joy and peace in
believing.[75] When we find our joy in life in joyous giving
to others for the sake of Christ, then we have gained
possession of the genuine Christmas spirit. For it is far
more blessed to give than to receive, and far more glad-
dening to make Christ rejoice in other men than to make
men rejoice without Christ.

Mary so radiant in your joy with your Son, Mary of the singing heart, Lady of the Magnificat, Mary, the Cause of our Joy, pray for us that we may become worthy of the promised eternal joy of Christ. O God, who through Your only-begotten Son our Lord Jesus Christ gladdens the whole world, grant us, we beg, through His Mother the Virgin Mary that we may come into possession of the joys of eternal life.[76] For this is heaven — an unending Christmas spent with You and Christ.

15. THE GRACE OF A MOTHER

MARY AT THE CRIB

Thoughts of the Madonna are sure to arise when we think of the Christ Child. As there are no babies without mothers, there is no Christ without Mary. We look for her when we visit any representation of the Christmas scene. We would be hurt by any one who would forget her presence with Him. Now that God has become Man, His mother will ever be near Him, and especially in His greatest needs during His baby days and His dying hours.

Artists have been deeply puzzled how to depict the

lovely looks of this maiden mother and her many-pointed beauty of character. Let us imagine her on the night of the divine birth. Her hours of waiting are ended; the time for His appearance has come. We know from the Church's teaching that, ever a virgin, she virginally conceived Christ and now virginally gives Him birth. She is alone for a space in the cave while Joseph tethers the animals or seeks firewood in the neighborhood. Then suddenly there are two. Without birth pains or physical distress, she now holds the Child in her arms. As light goes through glass without breaking it, so His flesh left hers intact. When God works a miracle in space and matter, when God is virginally born, why ask how He works His gracious wonders?

Let us lovingly watch her and listen to the Madonna of the stable. How shall one act toward a Son who is both God and yet a very tiny Boy needing a human mother's care? The urgency of His need comes first. She must wash Him in the salt-water bath and rub Him with powdered myrtle leaves, as her people were accustomed to do with the newborn. With deft, queenly grace in every movement, she picks up the garments nearby and wraps Him in the long linen bands which she had brought along from Galilee. She calls to Joseph to come see Him. As Joseph looks on, she kisses her Son very gently, her cheek against His cheek. It is the first human kiss that God has ever received and the best bit of human love that God has known since He made the world. Joseph smooths the hay bedding, and she lays Him in the manger. Joseph holds a cloak for her to put on and hangs the donkey's blanket to shield the cradled Child from any draughts. Together, she and he stand, holding each other's hands while their eyes glisten with surprised and grateful joy.

Now that His first bodily needs are cared for, she can

give some moments to thinking about Him. She sees only His human frame; but she believes that He is truly God. She must kneel; she must adore; she must welcome Him to earth; she must offer her lifelong service to His person. But He is also man. She offers a prayer to His Father for His welfare while He is under her charge. She begs that the cold night and open shed will not make Him ill. She offers a second prayer for Joseph. Then, as she kneels and fondles Him, she relaxes, smiling at the mystery, smiling at His beauty, smiling with the joy of being both a mother and a virgin. We who watch see "a beauty smile so that joy is in the eyes of all the saints."[77]

On His part, from His inner soul He pours forth on her the love of His human spirit. For unlike other children, He is born with active intellectual consciousness of all that pertains to His person and redemptive mission. It is easy to see why the little One loves this mother. God showed perfect taste in picking her and no other for His mother. Every proper exterior gift and interior grace consorted with the root grace of her divine maternity.

We watchers in the cave wonder what her thoughts are. In what words will she express her faith and hope in Him? In what sweet tones will she give Him divine honor and her human thanks? Will she repeat her own Magnificat in her exultant joy? Do the great prophecies of His advent come back to her? Does she promise to be a good mother to Him? As He stirs or cries a little, does she turn to Him as Man again and sing to Him her lullabies? Or is she just wordless, lost in wonder at the God that He is?

Observing her pray to Him in these first moments of His presence, we Catholics see at once that she is our model of thanksgiving after Holy Communion. We would like to learn from her how to greet and treat the God-Man when He comes to us.

Appreciating her wonderful success as His mother, our Catholic young understand how youthful virginity is their best preparation for the fruitfulness of parenthood.

MARY, THE MONSTRANCE

Not long after her first holy hour with Him, the hush of the silent midnight is broken as the angelic chorus rings in clear praise. Staffs beat on the trail and rocks clatter as the shepherds come. Now she has a new role to play. She who has been for nine months His tabernacle and ciborium as He hid within her must now be His monstrance, holding Him up for all who are interested in Him to see. After Joseph welcomes the shepherds and they see Him lying in the manger and have been introduced to His youthful mother, she lifts Him up to bless them. It is His first benediction. Her fingers and knees support the God of her heart; she is the Seat of Wisdom. Her smile wreaths Him with rays; she is the sun around whom most of His human joys will center. She watches the men of these hills stoop to their knees to adore Him and receive His blessing. She whispers glad thanks for their congratulations and hears them offer Joseph any help by which they may relieve the poverty of the Holy Family.

It is she who gives Him to the world. It is she who will give Christ to us. As she mothered Him, the Lord of grace, she mothers or mediates every grace that any man receives from Him.[78] She, too, will be the monstrance who after this exile shows unto us the blessed fruit of her womb, Jesus. All God's gracious glory comes to us through her; all man's gifts of glory go to Christ through her.

Blessed be her womb that gave Him flesh. Blessed be her spirit through which we come to spiritual birth. She is the mother through whom God became man; she somehow is the mother through whom we men become sons of God. The mother of His physical body is also the mother of His mystical body. We are her little ones whose spiritual good is born of her high motherhood. She is the mother whom our souls need for their care and guidance, for understanding and inspiration.

One of the permanent fruits of our Christmas celebrations should be our greater nearness to Christ. Herein we cannot do better than imitate Mary. Her graces of chastity, of love of children, of humble service in the home, of prayer, and of joy are accessible to all who would be like her and her Son. She will pray for us that we may become worthy of these promised graces of Christ.

THE CHRISTMAS ROSE

The living loveliness of Mary has suggested to many imaginations that she be likened to trees, fruits, and flowers. She has been called the jasmine, white and sweet. She is the Lady with the apple in her hand, for her Son is the apple of life to offset Eve's apple of death. She is the holly, as our English carol calls her:

> The holly bears a blossom
> As white as the lily flower,
> And Mary bore sweet Jesus Christ
> To be our Saviour.

> The holly bears a berry
> As red as any blood,
> And Mary bore sweet Jesus Christ
> To do poor sinners good.

> The holly bears a bark
> As bitter as any gall,
> And Mary bore sweet Jesus Christ
> For to redeem us all.[79]

The Church prays with the prophet that the earth would bud a Saviour. In another image, taken from Isaias[80] and adopted by St. Paul, the whole ancestry of Jesus is a tree or vine from the root of Jesse; Mary is the loveliest and freshest branch in the long line, and Christ is her fruit. Again, she has been named the Mystic Rose, and He who bloomed from her is the Christmas Rose. The eye leaps with surprise at seeing a Christmas rose flowering outdoors in the winter months. Its white, fresh flower with a mass of yellow stamens rises above the snow and after a few weeks turns to other shades. Its blossoming in December and its defiance of the cold and its contrast with the desolate garden about it make it a symbol of Christ. For He came at man's most undeserving hour, when men were yet enemies of God; He came to a very cold reception from earth; at that unexpected moment God so loved the world that He sent His only-begotten Son. He sent His Son, the Rose. For the rose is the flower of lovers and of martyrs. This Rose is the first flower in the new Paradise today recreated by a forgiving Father.

Prayer to Mary is a gift to Christ. Whatever we give to her we give to Him. Our thoughts, flowers, praises, beads, and requests are especially welcome when they reach Him through her hands. The Nativity seasonal hymn of the Church to the Mother of the Redeemer, *Alma Redemptoris Mater*, may be one of our most courteous ways of remembering what it means that Christ and sinners have a mother.

Darling Mother of the Redeemer,
Ever-open gate of heaven,
Constant star of the sea,
Hurry to aid your people
Who are falling yet struggling to rise.

To the astonishment of all nature
You brought into being the Creator of your own being.
O Virgin both before and after receiving
That glorious salute, that Ave of Gabriel,
Do have pity on us sinners.[81]

To this hymn the Church adds a prayer to our Mother:

Let us pray. O God, who conferred on the human race the
treasures of eternal salvation through the fruitful virginity of
Blessed Mary, graciously consent that we may experience that
our intercessor is this mother by whose merits we received the
very Author of life, our Lord Jesus Christ Your Son. Amen.

16. THE GRACE OF FRIENDLY ANGELS

HARK, THE HERALD ANGELS SING!
One of the charming details of the Nativity mystery is
the presence and activity of angels. One angel carried a
special prophecy to Zachary, who for his unbelief in the
message had to be punished by a period of dumbness.
Gabriel was the heavenly ambassador who won Mary's
consent to God's plan to become man. An angel visited
Joseph to explain Mary's virginal motherhood to him, as
well as to urge him to his marriage with her. Another citi-
zen of God's skies spoke to the bewildered shepherds and

95

then was joined by a singing host of the heavenly army.
Joseph and the Magi were warned of Herod's plotting
by other angels.

The angels act as servants of God and friends of men.
They are God's messengers, envoys bringing divine greetings and choristers of salvation's noel. They are diplomats
of God's court accredited to men, carriers of revelation,
and prudent counselors who help men find God. They
come by day and by night, to the wakeful and during
dreams. Their advent always marks a moment or a truth
of high importance. They move the thinking, willing, and
acting of the recipients of their trusted messages.

Though the purposeful visits of these personages from
another, nonmaterial world present many mysteries, we
feel that it was most fitting that angels should be par-
ticipants in the Christmas drama. The King of angels
had come to earth. It was right, then, that some of his
age-old spiritual subjects should come with Him. They
had seen His beauty as God in heaven; now they desired
to see His beauty as man on earth. They had learned that
His virgin mother was to be their queen; they must come
to pay court to her. They belong in heaven. But heaven
is centered on God, and now God is on earth. Therefore,
they belong on earth where the God of heaven now rests.
The tempting talk of angel enemies had begun man's doom
in Paradise. Our angel friends will begin our restoration
by preparing for the Incarnation and by announcing the
news. For ages they had been raising their adoring chants
to God's throne on high; tonight they will sing a new
song to God in motherly arms. They will be the links
between heaven and earth. They will see a nature lower
than their own that is yet greater than their own because
it is personally one with God's Word. They will see these
human beings whom God loves so much as to work these

many wonders for them and send His only-begotten Son
to them. They are the servants of God and will not cease
serving because God is on earth. Because they know that
service means loving what God loves, they will love and
help these poor men for whom God shows such fondness.

What if we had been members of the shepherd band
that first night when these creatures of light filled the
sky? We would have shivered with amazed fear, as they
did. We would have needed the deep-voiced comfort of
the angel of the Lord of Heaven: Fear not. For I bring
you and all the people most joyful tidings.[82] What is this
good news? It is the message which Israel and the human
race have been waiting for since the day of Adam and Eve's
expulsion: that today Christ, the Lord your Saviour is born
for you in the city of David. He? Alive? On earth? Nearby
us in Bethlehem? Born for our sake? For us poor shepherds? Then, having read their thoughts, the angel tells
them how to recognize the newly born Lord. You will
find the Infant wrapped in swaddling clothes and laid in
a manger. The message is complete in four sentences.

But this is a night for putting on a spectacle for these
friends of the Saviour. Suddenly, there was with the messenger a host of the heavenly army praising God and saying:
Glory to God on high, peace and good will to men on
earth.[83] The company was far more numerous than the
sheep on the rolling pastures about their watchmen. They
shattered the silence with their glorious music. Never
before nor since has such sweet polyphonic splendor been
heard on earth. We who have heard so many choirs try
to rival the angelic concert hope that they will repeat this
original Christmas program for us when our glorified bodies
are restored in heaven.

Surely, this is a new age. The old age of history had
begun with Adam's ashamed sobs as he fled the angel of

justice who was driving him from the scene of his sin. The new age of the kingdom of Christ's glory and peace begins with angel songs that invite shepherds to the scene of our salvation.

ACTING AS ANGELS

Our fancy adds many roles to those which the angels, by actual report of the evangelists, performed on Christmas night. We have seen them pictured as harpists accompanying their songs. We have imagined them as hurrying along with the shepherds as they moved down the slopes to visit the Child. We like to think of them hovering near Christ, dancing in His presence, humming to Him, rapturously adoring Him. We amuse ourselves by believing that some of them were little angels, just of the right size and right disposition to play with a human baby. We do well to believe that they remained invisibly near Christ during all His life on earth.

We should like not only to thank these angels for what they did for us at Christmas, but we should also like to imitate their way of serving the little King. Copying them at our human distance from them, we have adopted the widespread custom of sending Christmas greetings to relatives and friends afar. Each greeting card, visit, and telephone call is like the glad flash of an angel coming into another's life. Mailmen and Western Union messengers and telephone operators bring together God's friends as angels used to do.

From the angels we have learned to express our joy in swelling song. These Christmas songs are new songs, different songs, songs about God, songs about God's love, songs about redemption, cradle songs, love songs, folk songs, birthday songs, songs of peace, songs vibrant with joy, songs sparkling with light. They are not the old bitter songs that were warriors' shouts or drinking songs or dirges, songs of sin, of pain, or of dark earth. Christmas songs soar. Every voice joins the angels in glad welcome to Christ, to Mary, to Joseph. *Gloria in excelsis Deo.* And: "Holy, holy, Holy Lord. Heaven and earth are full of Thy glory. Blessed is He who comes in the name of the Lord." "Hail to the Lamb of God."

His Angels in Charge of Us

Christ's angel friends are friends also of all who desire to serve Christ. One of the comforting surplus gifts of our holy religion is the knowledge that in the struggle of life and in the fight for the right God has sent His angels to help us. Perhaps Gabriel was Mary's guardian angel. Perhaps the angelic chorus on Christmas night included the guardian angels of the shepherds. Perhaps all the guardian angels of all men were there for the greatest night in man's history. But whether our angels were present that night or not, they are certainly present near us this Christmas. They are friends, good spirits, both God's servants and our helpers. They are guardians, protecting us especially from spiritual evil. They see God in heaven and are trying to keep our faces turned in that heavenly direction. They are our brothers in grace under the headship of Christ and have true brotherly sentiments toward us. They are keepers of our consciences. They are engaged in deadly combat with the powers of evil rampant in the world. They are models to us of many virtues, of prayer, for instance, and speech, of zeal for Christ's truth and its spread among men, of joyous service to others, and of happiness of heart.

They speak to us and inspire us in their own secret way. Only those of us who are attuned catch their messages.

It is remarkable enough that their mighty canticle at Bethlehem was heard only by the shepherds, who alone had ears for the heralds. It is easy to be deaf to the angels' messages. For they are courteous spirits who respect our free will, who will try to advise us if we wish to hear counsel, but who will seldom, if ever, force themselves and their better views upon us. We must listen, invite their good words, and follow their lead. If we heed them, we will go over to see and adore this Wonder.

Guardian angels of our souls, let your glad wings guard our mail as it goes off to greet our dear ones. Let your bright voices inspire our own to sing heartily this Christmas. Hover over the children in our homes, as you once guarded the crib of Christ. Come, be with us during the Christmas Mass when your King and our Saviour is so close. Lift our minds from earth to heaven; lift our thoughts to Mary and to Christ. Stay with us until we find Christ the Lord on His throne and hear on high your eternal song of glory and peace.

Queen of the Angels, we beg you to direct our friendly angels in all their missions to our souls.

17. THE GRACE OF REMEMBRANCE

MARY'S HEART CHERISHED ALL THESE EVENTS

One of the clues in the Gospel of St. Luke indicating that the writer heard it from the Mother of the divine Child is the remark that Mary kept in her heart and pondered over all the wonders of the Christmas days. As closely as she had held His human body, so firmly she held the memories of these days in tender recollection. To her mother's heart every least fact touching her Son was a precious keepsake. Her grateful heart remembered for the sake of nourishing her spirit of thanksgiving to

101

God; her prayerful heart found light and joy in recalling the mysteries of the divine infancy. She is the model of all who pray before the crib. Later her memories served for the instruction of the Church and the preservation of the Holy Spirit's record of the Son of God.

The Church imitates Mary's fresh memory of the coming of her Son in the annual renewal of her Christmas liturgy. For she is the bride of Christ who has stored in her spirit all that pertains to her Bridegroom. The Church has many ways of reminding us of our Saviour's birth throughout the year: by the thrice-daily angelus, by encouraging the recitation of the joyous mysteries of the Rosary, by the display of the treasures of Christmas art in her places of worship, by feasts like the Annunciation and Maternity of Mary, and by reference to the Nativity and its graces in occasional Mass texts. But with the onset of Advent the Church quickens our expectations and urges our preparation for the new coming of her Spouse to earth. On Christmas Day her texts of the Divine Office and of the day's Masses revive the sweet memories of the days of Christ's conception, birth, and infancy.

But it is not in the crib scene, in the sermon, in prayers, and in hymns that the Church chiefly keeps His memory alive. It is in the sacrificial gift of the Mass, simply or splendidly offered, that the Church most of all remembers. For this is the memorial of all His marvels and mysteries, not only of His Passion and death, of His Resurrection and Ascension, but also of His first appearance to men in the beginnings of the cycle of the mysteries of the Incarnation.[84] For the Saviour, her High Priest, gave the Church this special power of remembering: Do this in memory of Me.[85] Copy what I am doing; that is, change bread and wine into my Body and Blood; offer Me; take Me and feast on Me. This is your remembrance of Me.

IN MEMORY OF ME

By a fortunate accident of speech, we who speak English have the most beautiful of all the names for this feast of Christ's birth. To us it is Christmas, the Mass of Christ. There is a beautiful series of partial likenesses between the events and the *dramatis personae* of the first Christmas and of our twentieth-century Christmas Mass.

In these Masses of the Nativity, Christ Himself is with us. He is here. He is come again. It is the same "true Body born of the Virgin Mary" which we hail with joy. It is the same second Person in God, God's Son and Mary's Son. It is the same Heavenly Visitor, our one and only Saviour, our King and Lord, our Light and Life, the Prince of our peace, the High Priest, and the Lamb of God. There is a difference in the condition of His Body and in the manner of His appearance; but all else is the same. His bodily state is no longer that of an infant with growth and suffering before Him. He is with us now as He is in heaven, the glorified, conquering, and crowned Christ. The manner of His appearance, too, is different. At Bethlehem, His humanity was visible and His divinity could not be seen except by faith. In the Mass, His humanity is also invisible, hidden together with His divinity under the appearances of mere bread and wine. But faith knows that He is the very same Christ, alive and wonderful, the Word made flesh dwelling in our company.

His purpose in coming in the Mass is in complete accord with His purpose in showing Himself on the first Christmas night. He is here to pardon our sins. He is here to flood our spirits with His angel-blinding Wisdom. He is here to make us sons of God, to share His sonship with us, and to give us His grace and peace. When during the sacrifice we repeat in the Creed: "For us and for our salvation He came down from heaven, became flesh of the Holy Spirit, was born of the Virgin Mary, and became man," we know that this same Christ is to be with us this Christmas Day for our redemption. It is an echo of the angels' revelation: To you is born a Saviour.

His Mass-life and Host-life show forth the same virtues that shone in the divine Child: lowliness, obedience to those who call Him from heaven, trust of His body and blood to men who will have Him as their spiritual food, the kindest love, the finest gift-giving heart, and the same noble poverty of the cave. To the glorious God and the splendid King of Heaven the richest furnishings of St. Peter's Basilica and altar must look pretty much like a shack. But He is content with it, if only He can be with us again.

In His Mass-life He is teaching the same basic lessons that He taught at Bethlehem: spiritual childhood, poverty of spirit, the need of sacrifice, willingness to forgive, hope in a Redeemer's help, and love of His Father.

The Christmas Sign

The Eucharist, like Christ, is a multiple sign: of reparation for the past, of the present gift of grace, and of pledged perfect happiness in heaven. The Eucharist resembles the Child in Simeon's arms: a sign of contradiction to unbelievers and a light of revealing truth to those who heed the call to come, believe, and adore. The Mass passes judgment on men. It is their greatest safety or their greatest danger. Men must choose to adore or ignore. The Mass makes the difference between men.

The manner of His coming and of His presentation of

Himself has overtones reminiscent of His original appearance. On that night He all of a sudden lay in His mother's arms, having slipped from the womb without pain or hurt to her; He was born, as it were, just by His own willing to be born. In the Mass upon the consecrating call of the priest, all of a sudden He is with us. Christ and the priest consecrate bread and wine together. It is Christ whom we hear in human words saying: "This is My Body." "This is My Blood."

The place has changed. He still comes in Bethlehem, but He also comes in thousands of other spots all over the world. Our church building becomes the Holy Land; our sanctuary, Judea; our altar, the cave; our corporal, chalice, and ciborium, the manger; and after Holy Communion our bodies cradle Him as Mary's arms did on that blessed night. But now He is everywhere where His priest has called for Him in the Mass. Christmas is everywhere, for Christ's Mass is in all lands.

The time may be midnight or any other hour. After centuries of expectancy, in the midst of silence, the almighty Word leaped down. Now after a short Advent of welcoming preparation, in the silence of the church, at the whispered consecrating words, Christ is with us. He stays a while with us in Holy Communion. He lingers with us in the Hosts kept in the tabernacle. He is with us all days even to the breakup of the world.

Besides the different manner of coming and of time, other physical circumstances differ. The cave in which He was born became a church because He was there; and our church becomes a Christmas cave because He is here. The veil of seeming bread and seeming wine cover Him now instead of swaddling clothes. Candles, torches of acolytes, sanctuary lamps, and electrical lights take the place of

the lantern of Joseph and the Magi's star. Trees from far
hills decorate the sanctuary and remind us of the hilly
pastures of the shepherds. The donkey that carried Mary
and the camels that bore the Magi have yielded to the
family car bringing the twentieth-century adorers to Christ.
But the Person who has come is the same!

The announcement of the Saviour's coming has taken a
new expression. Prophets had often predicted that He
would truly come. The Church throughout Advent and
especially on Christmas Eve pledged that He would come.
God does not send a new angel to declare His arrival,
but today appoints a deacon or priest to read the Christmas gospels to us. Our choirs and congregations sing with
the priest at the altar the very words of the Christmas
angels: *Gloria in Excelsis Deo!* Exultant organs and merry
bells join the jubilee of voices. All of us, acolytes and
worshiping congregation, are the shepherds who thrill to
the divine news.

THE HEART OF CHRISTMAS

Who are near Christ in the Mass? If Mary is near, we
cannot see her. The human priest is something of a
substitute for her. As she initiated the Incarnation by her
human co-operation with God's plan, the priest continues
the Incarnation by his anointed power of human co-
operation with God's mode of returning to earth. As she
showed Him to His visitors, the priest lifts Him for the
view of old and young. Our eyes are riveted on the raised
Host and Chalice, not on the image in the manger. For
this is He!

But it is not the priest alone who holds Christ. All of
us who receive His Body in Holy Communion become
other Marys and other Josephs, touching the Word made

flesh, kissing with our lips the beloved Saviour, and holding very close to our hearts the Heart of God made man.

The shepherds and Magi, Simeon and Anna, are now, doubtless, adoring Him in heaven. On earth we have taken their identity before His presence. Simple, poor souls represent the shepherds; the learned, wise, converts, and a few rich represent the Magi; little children represent the little ones of Bethlehem who died for Him; old folk represent the ancient Anna and Simeon. They were but a few; today we are millions. But by the favor of God some of their spirit is in our spirits. Like them, we offer faith in His Divinity, hope in His redeeming, love for His kindness. We tender our welcome and gifts. We wonder, we adore, we rejoice. We give thanks. We burn with desire for His present and eternal friendship. We offer Him whatever He wishes of what we have: our life, our blood, our wealth, our time, our service. We make our own the Church's prayer over us at the moment when we receive the Christ hidden in the Host: "May the Body of our Lord Jesus Christ preserve our souls for everlasting life." This is the Christmas gift we ask of Him.

Sadly enough, St. John's statement of His coming is also still true. Some still do not receive His light and grace. Many do not know Him; some others knowingly spurn Him. Some bring their children to the knees of Santa Claus, but do not lead them to the crib and altar of Christ. Maybe this ignorance of Christ and forgetfulness of Him is one more proof that it is really He who comes in the Mass.

The great grace of Christ's real presence on earth lives on in His real presence in the Blessed Sacrament. This is the greatest gift; this is a perpetual Christmas. No wonder that it keeps alive His memory. No wonder that a Christ-

mas spent with Christ is a Christmas whose very center
is the Lord of the Mass, the Christ on the altar, the
Christ in Holy Communion, the Christ visited in the
Tabernacle. We do Him the great courtesy of remembering Him in the way that He asked to be remembered:
"Do *this* in memory of Me." All other memorials of
Christ may be good and wonderful. But cherishing the
Eucharistic Christ is the best. It is the most intimate and
most real of contacts with Christ. It brings us unbelievably
close to Him, as Mary herself was. The Mass is the center
of all things at Christmas; for here is Christ, the Gift
of all gifts, the Center of all hearts, the Founder of Christmas, God and Man.

When He comes, we salute Him with His Apostle:
"My Lord and my God!"

Our Father in heaven, graciously take this Gift which
we, Your servants, offer You in memory of the birth of
Your Son who is our Lord Jesus Christ.

NOTES AND REFERENCES

1. *The Grace of Sonship*, pages 1–8.
   1. Cf. Lk. 1:35, 32.
   2. Cf. Lk. 1:43.
   3. Cf. Jn. 1:1, 3, 14.
   4. The title of G. K. Chesterton's book, *The Everlasting Man* (New York: Dodd, Mead, 1925). "Omnipotence in Bonds" is one of John Henry Cardinal Newman's sermons.
   5. Cf. Phil. 2:6, 7.
   6. Cf. H. Denzinger and others, *Enchiridion Symbolorum* (Friburg and Barcelona: Herder, 1952), 29th ed., nos. 143, 144.
   7. Cf. Jn. 1:11–14, 16.
   8. Cf. 1 Jn. 3:1; Gal. 3:26, 29; 4:4–7; Tit. 3:7; 1 Jn. 3:2; 4:6–10, and chapter 5.
   9. 2 Pet. 1:4.
   10. Joseph A. Jungmann, S.J., *The Mass of the Roman Rite: Its Origin and Development*, translated by Francis A. Brunner, C.Ss.R. (New York: Benziger, 1955), II, 63.
   11. Pius XII, *Mediator Dei* (New York: America Press, 1954), no. 155.
   12. Cf. Mt. 5:48.
   13. Cf. Eph. 5:1.

2. *The Grace of a Heavenly Visit*, pages 9–15.
   14. Cf. Jn. 1:11; Lk. 2:7.
   15. Cf. Tit. 3:4.
   16. Cf. Jn. 1:14; 1 Jn. 1:1–3.
   17. Cf. Lk. 2:29.
   18. Cf. Lk. 1:68.
   19. Cf. Mt. 25:35–36.
   20. Cf. Tit. 2:11–12.
   21. Alice Meynell, *Poems of Alice Meynell* (Westminster, Md.: Newman, 1955), Centenary ed., p. 35, "Unto us a Son is given."
   22. Cf. Collect of the Mass of the vigil of Christmas.

3. *The Grace of a Redeemer*, pages 16–21.
   23. Cf. Lk. 2:11.
   24. Cf. Mt. 1:21; Lk. 1:31.
   25. Cf. Jn. 1:29.
   26. Alice Meynell, *op. cit.*, p. 65, "Beyond Knowledge."
   27. Lk. 5:32.
   28. Jn. 15:5.
   29. Cf. Tit. 3:4.

30. Cf. Lk. 1:46–47.
31. Verse translation by J. M. Neale and others. Reprinted in Matthew Britt, O.S.B., *The Hymns of the Breviary and Missal* (New York: Benziger, 1922), pp. 100–101.

4. *The Grace of a King*, pages 22–28.

32. Cf. Jn. 18:33–37; Lk. 23:3; Mk. 15:2.
33. From Sedulius' hymn on the life of Christ.
34. Cf. Mt. 2:2.

5. *The Grace of Spiritual Childhood*, pages 29–35.

35. Cf. Mt. 18:3; Lk. 18:16–17.
36. *The Spiritual Exercises of St. Ignatius Loyola* (New York: Schaefer, 1904), "The Second Week: The Second Contemplation," p. 41.
37. Cf. Lk. 9:48.

6. *The Grace of Adoration*, pages 36–41.

38. Cf. Lk. 2:15.
39. Cf. Mt. 2:2, 11.
40. Joseph A. Jungmann, S.J., *op. cit.*, I, pp. 350–356 on the history of the Gloria and analysis of the text.

7. *The Grace of a Divine Call*, pages 42–47.

41. Cf. Hebr. 10:5–9; Ps. 39:8.
42. Cf. Lk. 1:38, 48.
43. Cf. Jn. 11:28.
44. Cf. 1 Kings 3:9–10.
45. Cf. Mt. 25:34.
46. Cf. Mt. 25:21, 23.

8. *The Grace of Poverty of Spirit*, pages 48–54.

47. Cf. 2 Cor. 8:9.
48. Cf. Blessed Robert Southwell's poem, "Come to your Heaven, you heavenly Choirs," reprinted in many anthologies, such as David Cecil, ed., *The Oxford Book of Christian Verse* (London: Oxford U. Press, 1941), pp. 70–71; F. J. Sheed, *Poetry and Life* (New York: Sheed, Ward, 1942), pp. 19–21.
49. Mt. 5:3. Further comment on poverty of spirit is given by St. Paul in 1 Timothy, chapter 6 with its exhortations to the rich.

9. *The Grace of a Birthday*, pages 55–59.

50. Isa. 9:6. It is used as *Introit* of the third Christmas Mass.
51. St. Leo I, fourth Christmas sermon.
52. Cf. Mk. 9:36; Mt. 25:40.
53. The ideas of old and new are played on in the Collect of the third Christmas Mass and the Postcommunion of the second Mass.

10. *The Grace of a Giving Heart*, pages 60–64.

54. Cf. Jn. 3:16; 1 Jn. 4:9–10; Isa. 9:6.

55. The Epistle is from Tit. 2:11–15.
56. Postcommunion of the third Christmas Mass.
57. Cf. Lk. 6:38.

11. *The Grace of Light*, pages 65–70.

58. Correggio's painting of the Holy Night is famous for this radiation of light from the Child.
59. Jn. 8:12; cf. Jn. 1:4–5, 9; 1 Jn. 1:5 and 3:19.
60. Cf. 2 Cor. 4:4–6.
61. Cf. Collect of the second Christmas Mass.
62. Cf. Collect of the feast of the Epiphany.
63. Cf. last two lines of St. Thomas Aquinas' poem, "Panis Angelicus."

12. *The Grace of the Shadow*, pages 71–76.

64. Cf. Hebr. 10:5–9; Ps. 39:8.
65. Cf. Hebr. 9:15–16; 10:18.
66. Hilda Graef, *The Scholar and the Cross* (Westminster, Md.: Newman, 1955), especially pp. 105–109.

13. *The Grace of Peace*, pages 77–81.

67. Isa. 9:6. The principal treatment of the peace of Christ is in Pope Pius XI, *Ubi Arcano Dei* (*The Peace of Christ in the Kingdom of Christ*), reprinted in Harry C. Koenig, ed., *Principles for Peace* (Washington: National Catholic Welfare Conference, 1943, distributed by Bruce, Milwaukee), nos. 758–823.
68. Shakespeare, *Hamlet*, Act I near end of Scene 1.
69. Mt. 5:9.
70. Third Agnus Dei of the Mass.

14. *The Grace of Joy*, pages 82–87.

71. Cf. Lk. 2:10–11.
72. Cf. Mt. 2:9–10.
73. Cf. Zach. 9:9. The original is better referred to Christ's entry on Palm Sunday.
74. Offertory chant of the first Christmas Mass.
75. Cf. Rom. 15:13.
76. This prayer is modified from the Marian prayer of the Paschal season that is used with the *Regina coeli*.

15. *The Grace of a Mother*, pages 88–94.

77. The phrase is Dante's.
78. Gerard Manley Hopkins, S.J., develops this idea in beautiful detail in his poem, "The Blessed Virgin Compared to the Air We Breathe." Cf. Robert Bridges and W. H. Gardner, ed., *Poems of Gerard Manley Hopkins* (New York: Oxford U. Press, 1948), 3rd ed. It is reprinted in many anthologies of religious and Marian poetry.
79. Many printings of this carol are available in books of carols and religious verse. Cf. David Cecil, ed., *The Oxford Book of Christian*

Verse (London: Oxford U. Press, 1941) and F. J. Sheed, *Poetry and Life* (New York: Sheed, Ward, 1942), pp. 22–23.

80. Cf. Isa. 11:1; Acts 13:22–23. Abbot Suger's famous Jesse tree so often copied in stained glass, for instance at Chartres, is described in Emile Mâle, *Religious Art from the Twelfth to the Eighteenth Century* (New York: Pantheon, 1949), 29–31.

81. Other versions in Sister M. Therese, ed., *I Sing of a Maiden* (New York: Macmillan, 1947), p. 44, which attributes the composition to Hermanus Contractus, 1013–1054; also in Matthew Britt, O.S.B., *The Hymns of the Breviary and the Missal* (New York: Benziger, 1922) which gives a rhymed version.

16. *The Grace of Friendly Angels*, pages 95–100.

82. Cf. Lk. 2:8–14.

83. For this translation which locates the idea of good will in God's selection rather than in man's preparation, see Joseph A. Jungmann, S.J., *op. cit.*, I, 351.

17. *The Grace of Remembrance*, pages 101–108.

84. Joseph A. Jungmann, S.J., *op. cit.*, II, 49–50 mentions earlier Mass texts of the prayer, *Suscipe, sancta Trinitas,* which explicitly included the Incarnation and Nativity with the present trilogy of the Passion, Resurrection, and Ascension formally memorialized in words in this prayer.

85. Cf. Lk. 22:19; 1 Cor. 11:24.

The Library of Congress has cataloged this publication as follows:

Wuellner, Bernard
    The graces of Christmas. Milwaukee, Bruce Pub. Co.
₁1958₎
    112 p. illus. 24 cm.

––––––––––

    1. Christmas—Meditations.   ɪ. Title.
BV45.W8   264.021   58–11570 ‡
Library of Congress